The Concise

TOWNSCAPE

Gordon Cullen

The Concise

TOWNSCAPE

VNR VAN NOSTRAND REINHOLD COMPANY
NEW YORK CINCINNATI TORONTO LONDON MELBOURNE

Van Nostrand Reinhold Company Regional Offices:
New York Cincinnati Chicago Millbrae Dallas

Van Nostrand Reinhold Company International Offices:
London Toronto Melbourne

Printed in Great Britain

Published by Van Nostrand Reinhold Company
A Division of Litton Educational Publishing, Inc.
450 West 33rd Street, New York, N.Y. 10001

CONTENTS

ACKNOWLEDGEMENTS

The author thanks the following for permission to reproduce photographs: Aerofilms on pages 46 bottom, 136 top left, 139 top; Agenzia Alinari, Rome, page 72, bottom right; the *Architectural Review* pages 26 top, 39 top, 41, 42 bottom, 44 both, 50 top and bottom right, 65 top, 70 top, 71 both, 75 top, 81 bottom, 93 bottom, 104, 123–6, 133 top and centre, 134 all except top left, 135, 136 all except top left, 145, 146 two bottom and centre right, 148, 149 top, and for illustrations by the following photographers: Dell & Wainwright page 18 left column, 40 top left, 78 top; Dewar Mills page 194 top; I. de Wolfe page 22 top, 23 bottom, 24 top and bottom left, 38, 51 both, 53 top, 54 top right and bottom right, 61 top, 76 both, 94 centre left, 103 bottom, 107–8, 109 top, 110, 129–131, 158 bottom left, 159 bottom, 161 bottom left, 177, 178 top and centre left, 181 both, 189–92, H.de Burgh Galwey pages 31 top, 32 bottom, 40 centre left, 58 top two, 61 bottom, 64 bottom, 79 bottom right, 87 right, 88 three bottom, and centre middle and right, 89 two bottom, 90 two bottom, 94 bottom right, 96 centre left, 112–6, 141–3, 178 top right, 179; Hastings page 96 right of centre and bottom centre; John Maltby page 40 bottom right; Ian McCallum pages 29 bottom left, 30 bottom, 36 bottom, 52 both, 53 bottom, 64 top, 68 bottom, 69 bottom, 82 bottom, 87 top left, 88 centre left, 90 top, 92 top, 94 centre right, 96 top centre and right, 158 top right, 160 two top, 161 top left, 171 top, 172, 176, 178 centre right; Ian Nairn pages 34 bottom, 35 top, 36 top, 47 right, 57 bottom, 58 second from bottom, 69 top, 73 top, 74 bottom; J M.Richards pages 79 top, 87 bottom left, 90 two left and bottom right, 96 top left, 161 top right; Sylvia Sayer page 60 top; W. J. Toomey pages 56, 58 bottom, 146 top right; also Black Star page 151 bottom; Oscar Bladh page 27 left; Charles Borup page 96 bottom right; Cracknell page 173 top; D'Andre Vigneau page 37 bottom; Eric de Maré pages 21, 23 top left, 46 top, 49 bottom, 66 top, 88 top left, 89 top; Entwistle page 78 bottom left; Fox Photos page 109 bottom; Marcel Gautherot pages 169–70; General Electric Co. page 146 top left; Hedrich Blessing page 161 bottom left; Hobbs, Ofen & Co. page 149 two bottom; Jack Howe page 188; H. Dennis Jones page 22 bottom; Jose do Patrocinio Andrade page 158 bottom right; C. and S. Kestin page 83 bottom; G. E. Kidder Smith pages 33 bottom, 83 top, 168 right, 171 bottom, 173 bottom, 174 both; Herbert List page 81 top left; Millar and Harris pages 42 top; the National Gallery page 28; S. W Newbery page 82 top; Cas Oorthuys page 23 right (reproduced from *This is London*, published by Bruno Cassirer); Photoflight page 134 top left; John Piper page 66 bottom, 95 bottom left; Poles Ltd., Birmingham page 146 centre left; Paul Popper page 168 centre left; Press and Publicity Photographic Co. page 139 bottom; A. E. Raddy pages 117, 119, 158 top left; Radio Times Hulton Picture Library page 48 bottom; Roads Campaign Council page 27 right; L. Sievking page 73 bottom; A. R. Sinsabaugh page 68 top; Spectrocolour page 96 bottom left; R. Stallard page 40 bottom left; Struwing page 37 top; *The Times* pages 47 left, 57 centre, 59 bottom, 77 both; Reece Winstone page 26 bottom. The remainder of the photographs were taken by the author.

All the drawings are by the author, but he would like to thank the Cambridge University Press for permission to reproduce the drawing on page 35 which appears in *The town of Cambridge as it ought to be Reformed* by David Roberts; and Messrs Methuen for the drawing on page 80 which is reproduced from *A Wanderer in London* by Ebbe Sadolin.

There are advantages to be gained from the gathering together of people to form a town. A single family living in the country can scarcely hope to drop into a theatre, have a meal out or browse in a library, whereas the same family living in a town can enjoy these amenities. The little money that one family can afford is multiplied by thousands and so a collective amenity is made possible. A city is more than the sum of its inhabitants. It has the power to generate a surplus of amenity, which is one reason why people like to live in communities rather than in isolation.

Now turn to the visual impact which a city has on those who live in it or visit it. I wish to show that an argument parallel to the one put forward above holds good for buildings: bring people together and they create a collective surplus of enjoyment; bring buildings together and collectively they can give visual pleasure which none can give separately.

One building standing alone in the countryside is experienced as a work of architecture, but bring half a dozen buildings together and an art other than architecture is made possible. Several things begin to happen in the group which would be impossible for the isolated building. We may walk through and past the buildings, and as a corner is turned an unsuspected building is suddenly revealed. We may be surprised, even astonished (a reaction generated by the composition of the group and not by the individual building). Again, suppose that the buildings have been put together in a group so that one can get inside the group, then the space created between the buildings is seen to have a life of its own over and above the buildings which create it and one's reaction is to say 'I am inside IT' or 'I am entering IT'. Note also that in this group of half a dozen buildings there may be one which through reason of function does not conform. It may be a bank, a temple or a church amongst houses. Suppose that we are just looking at the temple by itself, it would stand in front of us and all its qualities, size, colour and intricacy, would be evident. But put the temple back amongst the small houses and immediately its size is made more real and more obvious by the comparison between the two scales. Instead of being a big temple it TOWERS. The difference in meaning between bigness and towering is the measure of the relationship.

In fact there is an *art of relationship* just as there is an art of architecture. Its purpose is to take all the elements that go to create the environment: buildings, trees, nature, water, traffic, advertisements and so on, and to weave them together in such a way that drama is released. For a city is a dramatic event in the environment. Look at the research that is put into making a city work: demographers, sociologists, engineers, traffic experts; all co-operating to form the myriad factors into a workable, viable and healthy organization. It is a tremendous human undertaking.

And yet . . . if at the end of it all the city appears dull, uninteresting and soulless, then it is not fulfilling itself. It has failed. The fire has been laid but nobody has put a match to it.

Firstly we have to rid ourselves of the thought that the excitement and drama that we seek can be born automatically out of the scientific research and solutions arrived at by the technical man (or the technical half of the brain). We naturally accept these solutions, but are not entirely bound by them. In fact we cannot be entirely bound by them because the scientific solution is based on the best that can be made of the average: of averages of human behaviour, averages of weather, factors of safety and so on. And these averages do not give an inevitable result for any particular problem. They are, so to speak, wandering facts which may synchronize or, just as likely, may conflict with each other. The upshot is that a town could take one of several patterns and still operate with success, equal success. Here then we discover a pliability in the scientific solution and it is precisely in the *manipulation of this pliability* that the art of relationship is made possible. As will be seen, the aim is not to dictate the shape of the town or environment, but is a modest one: simply to *manipulate within the tolerances*.

This means that we can get no further help from the scientific attitude and that we must therefore turn to other values and other standards.

We turn to the *faculty of sight*, for it is almost entirely through vision that the environment is apprehended. If someone knocks at your door and you open it to let him in, it sometimes happens that a gust of wind comes in too, sweeping round the room, blowing the curtains and making a great fuss. Vision is somewhat the same; we often get more than we bargained for. Glance at the clock to see the time and you see the wallpaper, the clock's carved brown mahogany frame, the fly crawling over the glass and the delicate rapier-like pointers. Cézanne might have made a painting of it. In fact, of course, vision is not only useful but it evokes our memories and experiences, those responsive emotions inside us which have the power to disturb the mind when aroused. It is this unlooked-for surplus that we are dealing with, for clearly if the environment is going to produce an emotional reaction, with or without our volition, it is up to us to try to understand the three ways in which this happens.

1. Concerning OPTICS. Let us suppose that we are walking through a town: here is a straight road off which is a courtyard, at the far side of which another street leads out and bends slightly before reaching a monument. Not very unusual. We take this path and our first view is that of the street. Upon turning into the courtyard the new view is revealed instantaneously at the point of turning, and this view remains with us whilst we walk across the courtyard. Leaving the courtyard we enter the further street. Again a new view is suddenly revealed although we are travelling at a uniform speed. Finally as the road bends the monument swings into view. The significance of all this is that although the pedestrian walks through the town at a uniform speed, the scenery of towns is often revealed in a series of jerks or revelations. This we call SERIAL VISION.

Examine what this means. Our original aim is to manipulate the elements of the town so that an impact on the emotions is achieved. A long straight road has little impact because the initial view is soon digested and becomes monotonous. The human mind reacts to a contrast, to the difference between things, and when two pictures (the street and the courtyard) are in the mind at the same time, a vivid contrast is felt and the town becomes visible in a deeper sense. It comes alive through the drama of juxtaposition. Unless this happens the town will slip past us featureless and inert.

There is a further observation to be made concerning Serial Vision. Although from a scientific or commercial point of view the town may be a unity, from our optical viewpoint we have split it into two elements: the *existing view* and the *emerging view*. In the normal way this is an accidental chain of events and whatever significance may arise out of the linking of views will be fortuitous. Suppose, however, that we take over this linking as a branch of the art of relationship; then we are finding a tool with which human imagination can begin to mould the city into a coherent drama. The process of manipulation has begun to turn the blind facts into a taut emotional situation.

2. Concerning PLACE. This second point is concerned with our reactions to the position of our body in its environment. This is as simple as it appears to be. It means, for instance, that when you go into a room you utter to yourself the unspoken words 'I am outside IT, I am entering IT, I am in the middle of IT'. At this level of consciousness we are dealing with a range of experience stemming from the major impacts of exposure and enclosure (which if taken to their morbid extremes result in the

symptoms of agoraphobia and claustrophobia). Place a man on the edge of a 500-ft. cliff and he will have a very lively sense of position, put him at the end of a deep cave and he will react to the fact of enclosure.

Since it is an instinctive and continuous habit of the body to relate itself to the environment, this sense of position cannot be ignored; it becomes a factor in the design of the environment (just as an additional source of light must be reckoned with by a photographer, however annoying it may be). I would go further and say that it should be exploited.

Here is an example. Suppose you are visiting one of the hill towns in the south of France. You climb laboriously up the winding road and eventually find yourself in a tiny village street at the summit. You feel thirsty and go to a nearby restaurant, your drink is served to you on a veranda and as you go out to it you find to your exhilaration or horror that the veranda is cantilevered out over a thousand-foot drop. By this device of the containment (street) and the revelation (cantilever) the fact of height is dramatized and made real.

In a town we do not normally have such a dramatic situation to manipulate but the principle still holds good. There is, for instance, a typical emotional reaction to being below the general ground level and there is another resulting from being above it. There is a reaction to being hemmed in as in a tunnel and another to the wideness of the square. If, therefore, we design our towns from the point of view of the moving person (pedestrian or car-borne) it is easy to see how the whole city becomes a plastic experience, a journey through pressures and vacuums, a sequence of exposures and enclosures, of constraint and relief.

Arising out of this sense of identity or sympathy with the environment, this feeling of a person in street or square that he is in IT or entering IT or leaving IT, we discover that no sooner do we postulate a HERE than automatically we must create a THERE, for you cannot have one without the other. Some of the greatest townscape effects are created by a skilful relationship between the two, and I will name an example in India, where this introduction is being written: the approach from the Central Vista to the Rashtrapathi Bhawan[1] in New Delhi. There is an open-ended courtyard composed of the two Secretariat buildings and, at the end, the Rashtrapathi Bhawan. All this is raised above normal ground level and the approach is by a ramp. At the top of the ramp and in front of the axis building is a tall screen of railings. This is the setting. Travelling through it from the Central Vista we see the two Secretariats in full, but the Rashtrapathi Bhawan is partially

[1] The President's Residence, lately Viceregal Lodge.

hidden by the ramp; only its upper part is visible. This effect of truncation serves to isolate and make remote. The building is withheld. We are Here and it is There. As we climb the ramp the Rashtrapathi Bhawan is gradually revealed, the mystery culminates in fulfilment as it becomes immediate to us, standing on the same floor. But at this point the railing, the wrought iron screen, is inserted; which again creates a form of Here and There by means of the screened vista. A brilliant, if painfully conceived, sequence[2] (illustration, page 20).

3. Concerning CONTENT. In this last category we turn to an examination of the fabric of towns: colour, texture, scale, style, character, personality and uniqueness. Accepting the fact that most towns are of old foundation, their fabric will show evidence of differing periods in its architectural styles and also in the various accidents of layout. Many towns do so display this mixture of styles, materials and scales.

Yet there exists at the back of our minds a feeling that could we only start again we would get rid of this hotchpotch and make all new and fine and perfect. We would create an orderly scene with straight roads and with buildings that conformed in height and style. Given a free hand that is what we might do . . . create symmetry, balance, perfection and conformity. After all, that is the popular conception of the purpose of town planning.

But what is this conformity? Let us approach it by a simile. Let us suppose a party in a private house, where are gathered together half a dozen people who are strangers to each other. The early part of the evening is passed in polite conversation on general subjects such as the weather and the current news. Cigarettes are passed and lights offered punctiliously. In fact it is all an exhibition of manners, of how one ought to behave. It is also very boring. This is conformity. However, later on the ice begins to break and out of the straightjacket of orthodox manners and conformity real human beings begin to emerge. It is found that Miss X's sharp but good-natured wit is just the right foil to Major Y's somewhat simple exuberance. And so on. It begins to be fun. Conformity gives way to the agreement to differ within a recognized tolerance of behaviour.

Conformity, from the point of view of the planner, is difficult to avoid but to avoid it deliberately, by creating artificial diversions, is surely worse than the original boredom. Here, for instance, is a programme to rehouse 5,000 people. They are all treated the same, they get the same kind of house. How *can* one differentiate? Yet if we start from a much wider point of view we will see that tropical housing differs from tem-

[2] It was the cause of bitterness between Lutyens and Baker.

perate zone housing, that buildings in a brick country differ from buildings in a stone country, that religion and social manners vary the buildings. And as the field of observation narrows, so our sensitivity to the local gods must grow sharper. There is too much insensitivity in the building of towns, too much reliance on the tank and the armoured car where the telescopic rifle is wanted.

Within a commonly accepted framework—one that produces lucidity and not anarchy—we can manipulate the nuances of scale and style, of texture and colour and of character and individuality, juxtaposing them in order to create collective benefits. In fact the environment thus resolves itself into not conformity but the interplay of This and That.

It is a matter of observation that in a successful contrast of colours not only do we experience the harmony released but, equally, the colours become more truly themselves. In a large landscape by Corot, I forget its name, a landscape of sombre greens, almost a monochrome, there is a small figure in red. It is probably the reddest thing I have ever seen.

Statistics are abstracts: when they are plucked out of the completeness of life and converted into plans and the plans into buildings they will be lifeless. The result will be a three-dimensional diagram in which people are asked to live. In trying to colonize such a wasteland, to translate it from an environment for walking stomachs into a home for human beings, the difficulty lay in finding the point of application, in finding the gateway into the castle. We discovered three gateways, that of motion, that of position and that of content. By the exercise of vision it became apparent that motion was not one simple, measurable progression useful in planning, it was in fact two things, the Existing and the Revealed view. We discovered that the human being is constantly aware of his position in the environment, that he feels the need for a sense of place and that this sense of identity is coupled with an awareness of elsewhere. Conformity killed, whereas the agreement to differ gave life. In this way the void of statistics, of the diagram city, has been split into two parts, whether they be those of Serial Vision, Here and There or This and That. All that remains is to join them together into a new pattern created by the warmth and power and vitality of human imagination so that we build the home of man.

That is the theory of the game, the background. In fact the most difficult part lies ahead, the Art of Playing. As in any other game there are recognized gambits and moves built up from experience and precedent. In the pages that follow an attempt is made to chart these moves under the three main heads as a series of cases

New Delhi 1959

INTRODUCTION TO 1971 EDITION

In writing an introduction to this edition of *Townscape* I find little to alter in the attitude expressed in the original introduction written ten years ago.

It has been said that a new edition of *Townscape* should rely on modern work for its examples instead of these being culled from the past. This has not been done for two reasons.

Firstly the task of finding the sharp little needles in the vast haystack of post-war building would be quite uneconomical. This leads to the second point, why should it be so difficult? Because, in my view, the original message of *Townscape* has not been delivered effectively.

We have witnessed a superficial civic style of decoration using bollards and cobbles, we have seen traffic-free pedestrian precincts and we have noted the rise of conservation.

But none of these is germane to townscape. The sadness of the situation is that the superficials have become the currency but the spirit, the Environment Game itself, is still locked away in its little red and gilt box.

The position may indeed have deteriorated over the last ten years for reasons which are set out below.

Man meets environment: unfamiliarity, shock, ugliness and boredom according to what kind of man you are. The problem is not new but is this generation getting more than its fair share? Yes. Reason? The reason in my view is the speed of change which has disrupted the normal communication between planner and planee. The list is familiar enough: more people, more houses, more amenities, faster communications and unfamiliar building methods.

The speed of change prevents the environment organisers from settling down and learning by experience how to humanise the raw material thrown at them. In consequence the environment is ill-digested. London is suffering from indigestion. The gastric juices, as represented by planners, have not been able to break down all the vast chunks of hastily swallowed stodge into emotional nutriment. We may be able to do many things our grandparents could not do but we cannot digest any faster. The process, be it in stomach or brain, is part of our human bondage. And so we have to make organisational changes in order that human scale can be brought into effective contact with the forces of development.

The critical
point where the
big column
lets the
slender column
pass

Sées

The first change is to popularise the art of environment on the principle that the game improves with the amount of popular emotion invested and this is the crux of the situation. The stumbling block here is that in the popular mind administrative planning is dull, technical and forbidding whilst good planning is conceived as a wide, straight street with bushy-topped trees on either side, full stop. On the contrary! The way the environment is put together is potentially one of our most exciting and widespread pleasure sources. It is no use complaining of ugliness without realising that the shoes that pinch are really a pair of ten-league boots.

How to explain? Example: the nearest to hand at the time of writing is Sées cathedral near Alençon, p.14. The Gothic builders were fascinated by the problem of weight, how to support the culmination of their structures, the vault, and guide its weight safely down to earth. In this building weight has been divided into two parts. The walls are supported by sturdy cylindrical columns: the vault itself, the pride of the endeavour, appears to be supported on fantastically attenuated applied columns which act almost as lightning conductors of gravity between heaven and the solid earth. The walls are held up by man, the vault is clearly held up by angels. 'I understand weight, I am strong', 'I have overcome weight, I am ethereal'. 'We both spring from the same earth together, we need each other'. Through the centuries they commune together in serenity.

As soon as the game or dialogue is understood the whole place begins to shake hands with you. It bursts all through the dull business of who did what and when and who did it first. We know who did it, it was a chap with a twinkle in his eye.

This is the Environment Game and it is going on all round us. You will see that I am not discussing absolute values such as beauty, perfection, art with a big A, or morals. I am trying to describe an environment that chats away happily, plain folk talking together. Apart from a handful of noble exceptions our world is being filled with system-built dumb blondes and a scatter of Irish confetti. Only when the dialogue commences will people stop to listen.

Until such happy day arrives when people in the street throw their caps in the air at the sight of a planner (the volume of sardonic laughter is the measure of your deprivation) as they now do for footballers and pop singers, a holding operation in two parts will be necessary.

First, streaming the environment. It is difficult to fight for a general principle, easier to protect the particular. By breaking down the environment into its constituent parts the ecologist can fight for his national parks, local authority for its green belts, antiquarians for conservation areas and so on. This is already happening.

Second, the time scaling of these streams. Change, of itself, is often resented even if it can be seen to be a change for the better. Continuity is a desirable characteristic of cities. Consequently while planning consent in a development stream might be automatic one may have to expect a built-in delay of ten or even twenty years in an important conservation area. This is not necessarily to improve the design but simply to slow down the process. This also is happening, if grudgingly, in the case of Piccadilly Circus.

But the main endeavour is for the environment makers to reach their public, not democratically but emotionally. As the great Max Miller once remarked across the footlights on a dull evening 'I know you're out there, I can hear you breathing'.

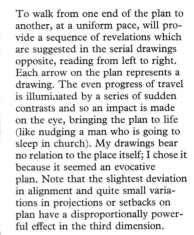

To walk from one end of the plan to another, at a uniform pace, will provide a sequence of revelations which are suggested in the serial drawings opposite, reading from left to right. Each arrow on the plan represents a drawing. The even progress of travel is illuminated by a series of sudden contrasts and so an impact is made on the eye, bringing the plan to life (like nudging a man who is going to sleep in church). My drawings bear no relation to the place itself; I chose it because it seemed an evocative plan. Note that the slightest deviation in alignment and quite small variations in projections or setbacks on plan have a disproportionally powerful effect in the third dimension.

IPSWICH 1, 2

3, 4

These three sequences, Oxford, Ipswich and Westminster, try to recapture in the limited and static medium of the printed page a little of the sense of discovery and drama that we experience in moving through towns. Oxford; the cube, 1, the drum, 3, and the cone, 4, create an unfolding drama of solid geometry. This is the unfolding of a mystery, the sense that as you press on more is revealed. Ipswich; a modest archway performs the office of dividing the prospect into two things, the street you are in and the place beyond, into which you emerge so that you move out of one ambience into another. Westminster; the shifting interplay of towers, spires and masts, all the intricacy of fresh alignments and grouping, the shafts of penetration and the sudden bunching of emphatic verticals into a dramatic knot, these are the rewards of the moving eye, but an eye which is open and not lazy.

1

2

3

4

5

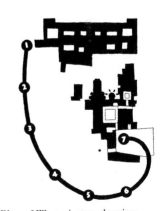

Plan of Westminster, showing
6, 7 viewpoints

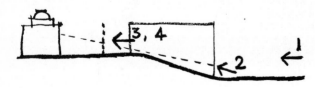

The sequence in New Delhi (read the photographs from left to right) emphasizes the role of levels and screening in serial vision, for here what could simply have been one picture reproduced four times, each view enlarging the centre of the previous view and bringing us near to the terminal building, turns out to be four separate and unique views (see description in the Introduction).

PLACE

possession

In a world of black and white the roads are for movement and the buildings for social and business purposes. Yet since most people do just what suits them when it suits them, we find that the out-of-doors is colonized for social and business purposes. Occupied territory, advantage, enclosure, focal point, indoor landscape, and so on, are all forms of possession, as the next seven pages show.

occupied territory (facing page)

Shade, shelter, amenity and convenience are the usual causes of possession. The emphasizing of such places by some permanent indication serves to create an image of the various kinds of occupation in the town, so that instead of a completely streamlined and fluid out-of-doors a more static and occupied environment

is created, like the ones shown opposite where a periodic occupation (chatting after church ?) is woven permanently into the town pattern by means of floorscape. The furniture of possession includes floorscape, posts, canopies, enclaves, focal points and enclosures. Although the amount of possession may be small yet its perpetuation in the furniture gives the town humanity and intricacy in just the same way that louvres on windows give texture and scale to a building even when the sun is not shining.

possession in movement

But static possession is only one aspect of the human grip on the out-of-doors and the next stage is to consider possession in movement. In the accompanying illustration the church walk is a definite thing having a well-defined beginning and end with a well-defined character; and this may be possessed while moving through it just as surely as the village cross may be by a villager sitting on its steps.

advantage

Again there are lines of advantage which can be colonized; the line along the parapet of a bridge which people seem to prefer for the sake of the immediacy of its view and position is one such (see also line of life p. 111).

viscosity

Where there is a mixture of static possession and possession in movement we find what may be termed viscosity, the formation of groups chatting, of slow window-shoppers, people selling newspapers, flowers and so on. The overhanging blinds, the space enclosed by the portico and the meandering character of the street provide the proper setting which may be compared to the picture below. Windswept and inhospitable, it emphasizes the segregation of outside and inside.

enclaves

The enclave or interior open to the exterior and having free and direct access from one to the other is seen here as an accessible place or room out of the main directional stream, an eddy in which footsteps echo and the light is lessened in intensity. Set apart from the hurly-burly of traffic, it yet has the advantage of commanding the scene from a position of safety and strength.

enclosure

Enclosure sums up the polarity of legs and wheels. It is the basic unit of the precinctual pattern; outside, the noise and speed of impersonal communication which comes and goes but is not of any place. Inside, the quietness and human scale of the square, quad or courtyard. This is the end product of traffic, this is the place to which traffic brings you. Without enclosure traffic becomes nonsense.

25

focal point

Coupled with enclosure (the hollow
object) as an artifact of possession, is
the focal point, the vertical symbol of
congregation. In the fertile streets
and market places of town and village
it is the focal point (be it column or
cross) which crystallizes the situation,
which confirms 'this is the spot'.
'Stop looking, it is here.' This mag-
nificent clarity illuminates many a
community but in many others the
chief function of the focal point has
been stripped away by the swirl and
hazards of traffic so that it becomes
merely an indifferent piece for the
antiquarian's notebook.

precincts

Left, in this significant picture, can be seen the whole urban pattern as it was and to some extent still is. Inside is the tightly built-up pedestrian town with its enclosures and no doubt areas of viscosity, its focal points and enclaves. Outside are the expressways for car and lorry, train and ship which exist to serve and vitalize the precincts. This is the traditional pattern at its clearest. The small photograph below shows some of these elements at their most disorganized, the chaotic mixture of houses and traffic in which both pedestrians and traffic suffer a diminution of their proper character.

indoor landscape and outdoor room

This is the watershed. Up to this point we have presented the environment as occupied territory serving the legitimate social and business needs of people and irrigated by traffic routes. Now arises the natural corollary that if the outdoors is colonized then the people who do this will attempt to humanize the landscape in just the same way they already do for the interiors. At this point we can find little difference between the two, and the terms Indoor Landscape and Outdoor Room make sense. In the top picture can be seen the patterned pavement (floorscape) and arcade. Over this is a building in which a man lives whilst the vault of the sky spans over. To the right an avenue of trees leads out to the hills. Here in this picture of an interior is all the spatial quality of a landscape. Below, the diners are gathered together under the ceiling lights and the Houses of Parliament sit on the perimeter like a model on the mantelpiece.

We cannot draw back. If the outdoors is to be colonized architecture is not enough. The outdoors is not just a display of individual works of architecture like pictures in a gallery, it is an environment for the complete human being, who can claim it either statically or in movement. He demands more than a picture gallery, he demands the drama that can be released all around him from floor, sky, buildings, trees and levels by the art of arrangement.

the outdoor room and enclosure

In this section of the casebook we are concerned with the person's sense of position, his unspoken reaction to the environment which might be expressed as 'I am in IT or above IT or below IT, I am outside IT, I am enclosed or I am exposed'. These

sensations are basically interlocked with human behaviour and their morbid expression is demonstrated in claustrophobia and agoraphobia. Enclosure or the outdoor room is, perhaps, the most powerful, the most obvious, of all the devices to instil this sense of position, of identity with the surroundings. It embodies the idea of HERENESS (which in the next five pages will be seen also to include multiple enclosure, space, looking out, etc.). The two exits to the same square in Bordeaux, above, provide an object lesson in how to preserve enclosure or how to let the sense of Hereness leak away into the remote distance. Left, a near-perfect example of the outdoor room with three-dimensional wallpaper.

multiple enclosure

From simple enclosure it is a step to the spatial variations which spring from this fertile form. The illustration shows two courtyards, the one we are in and the one beyond, divided by a third enclosure, the cloister. Thus there are three separate enclosures combined into one inter-penetrating whole.

block house

Here the dynamic curves of movement are held in suspense by the rectangular building which blocks the exit and so draws a momentary balance between enclosure and pure fluidity. It does not impede the flow of traffic or people but acts as a mark of punctuation or closure (which see on pp. 45 and 47).

insubstantial space

By dissolving the walls of enclosure with either screen, mirror or illusion, an intangible space is created which seems to have the property of receding as one advances and closing up behind. The sense of space is not particularized by the enclosing walls but exists throughout like a scent which hovers in a particular place. This is probably the most acute expression of that emotive force. The two examples given here, a London gin palace and the Oxford Museum in Oxford, need little explanation save to add that in the museum the instructive skeletons add to the general feeling of interpenetrating space.

defining space

It is sometimes astonishing how fragile can be the means of establishing enclosure or space. A wire stretched from wall to wall like a pencil stroke, a square of canvas stretched out overhead. In Chandigarh I saw a bustee, or collection of mud and thatch dwellings, arranged in the shade of three large trees alone in the plain. The space thus enclosed by the three trees became the civic space of the tiny community. In these pictures of the French Riviera and a restaurant at the Festival of Britain we see how bamboo is used to establish enclosure and space and how it achieves that evocative charm of containing whilst revealing what is beyond.

looking out of enclosure

Having established the fact of Hereness, the feeling of identity with a place, it is clear that this cannot exist of itself but must automatically create a sense of Thereness, and it is in the manipulation of these two qualities that the spatial drama of relationship is set up. These two examples demonstrate the primary reaction; in the case of Bath, left, the view beyond comes as an extra dimension and the trees inside the garden in Sweden have not the same kind of wildness as the tree beyond the wall. It is There.

thereness

These two pictures try to isolate the quality of Thereness which is lyrical in the sense that it is perpetually out of our reach, it is always There. The sea wall at Aldeburgh carries the shadows of houses, the shadows of warmth and laughter. Beyond is the great emptiness. In the wild country-side of Scotland the distance is made personal to us by the extension outwards of the roadside wall as a thin white line which, because of its meaning (possible line of travel), projects us out into the wilderness.

here and there

The first category of relationships
(pinpointing, change of level, vistas,
narrows, closure, etc.) is concerned
with the interplay between a known
here and a known there. The second
category, starting on p. 49, will be concerned with a known here and an
unknown there.

In Nash's Regent's Park terrace,
top, the dividing archway serves to
give the single composition intricacy
and growth. Judging by the in-
ordinate height of the archway we
are meant to see out of the relatively
modest courtyard up to the noble
main façade. He is playing off one
part of the composition against the
other in order to intensify the total
effect. My visualization, bottom, of
Hawksmoor's plan for Cambridge
includes this scene looking from
Great St Mary's along a reformed
Trinity Street. Here we are looking
from Hawksmoor's great forum into
another place whose individuality,
direction and character is unequivo-
cally stated by the two monuments.
By contrast the street today winds
quietly past the Senate House and
unobtrusively folds itself away. (This
is not intended as a choice between
the two but only to demonstrate
the visual impact of Hawksmoor's
scheme.)

In this example of housing in Cornwall there is a linear vibration between the two identities, that of the tree-lined road and the houses which are beyond and partly hidden by the sloping verge. Comparing this with a typical housing development along the roadside in which the houses are opened up to the road, its advantage is apparent. For not only are the houses divided from the road but also they appear to be. The road is one landscape element whilst the houses are a quite different element which happens, at this point, to be fairly close to the other.

looking into enclosure

Anything that may be occupied either by oneself or by one's imagination, which here lifts us into a carved stone aedicule (in Valencia), becomes to that extent of interest a warm colour in the greys of the inhospitable. Porticos, balconies and terraces have this ability to communicate. They draw us outwards.

pinpointing

The illumination halfway up the structure draws our attention outward and upward. What is this mystery of the commonplace? At least it takes our eyes off our toe-caps. Even the most ordinary means can be harnessed to the task of arousing in us the sense of otherness through the use of light, through pointing the finger. It is not the thing pointed out but the evocative act of pointing that arouses the emotions.

truncation

Foreground cuts out background and the normal, prosaic recession is disturbed. Instead of seeing the building in its elevational completeness, standing back but upon the same plane as one stands on oneself, the insistence of the foreground is intensified and from there to the building is a leap, a sudden visual break since the intervening floor (marked with objects which aid the effect of gradual recession) is cut out and the two things, foreground and distance, are brought into dramatic juxtaposition. So, instead of the scene making a gradual transition along the scale of distance between oneself and the distant object, this effect neatly juxtaposes the near and the distant. The two examples of truncation shown here, Versailles and a street in Holland,

37

suffice to demonstrate the charms of this immediacy. A somewhat similar effect is produced in those cases where a structure is separated from the viewer by a featureless plane, a great empty stretch which has no grip on the eye, such as the view of the Horse Guards from St James's Park or the view of the Supreme Court in Chandigarh across the wide lake.

change of level

Any account of one's emotional reactions to position must include the subject of levels. Below level produces intimacy, inferiority, enclosure and claustrophobia, above level gives exhilaration, command, superiority, exposure and vertigo; the act of descending, implies going down into the known and the act of ascending implies going up into the unknown. There is the strange correspondence of similar levels across a deep gap, near but remote, or the functional use of levels to join or separate the activities of various road users. This illustration shows the graveyard below Liverpool Cathedral, a quiet, meandering footpath beneath the immense weight of cliff and tower.

netting

Like truncation, this serves to link
the near with the remote. Just as the
carefully handled net held in the hand
captures the remote butterfly, so the
device of framing brings the distant
scene forward into the ambience of
our own environment by particulari-
zing, by making us see in detail
through having such detail brought
to our attention through the act of
netting. The applications of this will
be obvious in bringing the distant
land or townscape to life, in selecting
and rejecting to a purpose. One
thinks of the view of the Duke of
York's column with the towers of
Westminster behind, the whole scene
below eye level, netted by the arches
of Regent Street. Behind this and
similar cases lies the central fact that
the environment is one whole and
that all these devices are part of the
art of linking and joining that whole
into a significant pattern rather than
allowing it to remain a disjointed and
petty chaos.

These examples show the seafront
at Hove turned into a mural, and an
Italian allegorical scene in which the
captured ships underline the point.

silhouette

Silhouette may be valued for such classic examples of delicacy and refinement as this scene in Oxford, but the underlying function of such a perfect example remains to be revealed. By now we are all pretty well conversant with the slab block building with its uncompromising roof line, and it is recognized that this line divides too harshly the environment into the earth-bound structures and the airy volumes of the sky, whereas the tracery, the filigree, the openwork ridge capping all serve to net the sky, so that as the building soars up into the blue vault it also captures it and brings it down to the building. This capacity to net the sky is particularly rewarding in the fog and mists of England. Of the examples shown here it may be said that the roof structures of Corbusier, bottom left, and at Golden Lane, centre left, are to some extent a modern version of the classical filigree and delicacy and seek to entrap the space of the sky itself rather more wholeheartedly than the offices in Upper St Martin's Lane, below.

grandiose vista

Of the gambits used to exploit Here and There the vista is, of course, one of the most popular. The Grandiose vista does just what the whitewashed wall did in Scotland, p. 34, but in its own expensive way. It links you, in the foreground at Versailles, to the remote landscape, thus producing a sense of power or omnipresence.

division of space

In considering vistas or any linear extension it is interesting to note that the optical division of such a line into here and there should be done by bisecting the angle of vision into two roughly equal parts and not by dividing the line into two equal lengths. This is demonstrated in the diagram.

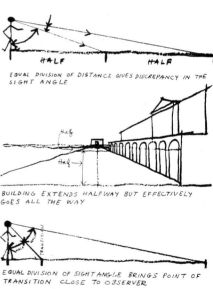

EQUAL DIVISION OF DISTANCE GIVES DISCREPANCY IN THE SIGHT ANGLE

BUILDING EXTENDS HALFWAY BUT EFFECTIVELY GOES ALL THE WAY

EQUAL DIVISION OF SIGHT ANGLE BRINGS POINT OF TRANSITION CLOSE TO OBSERVER

screened vista

This operates in the normal way except that the sense of Hereness is increased by the screen of foliage and the outside world made correspondingly remote.

41

To continue the Screened Vista, this example of St Paul's seen from Cheapside shows the use of foliage to withhold a view until one has penetrated past the tree when, quite suddenly, the great wall of the cathedral is revealed at close quarters with the dome almost vertically above. This dramatic impact at close range is only possible by withholding the view.

handsome gesture

Considering that so much of urban landscape consists of the quiet street, the simple backwater, the humdrum and ordinary, it is perhaps useful to utilize to the full what local talent there is, as this modest little scene shows. A fine display of, I hope, gilt lettering to illuminate the narrow street.

closed vista

Probably the most banal of all the Beaux Arts gambits is the closed vista, which puts a building down and then invites you to step back and admire it. This is a somewhat inorganic and purely architectural attitude, but the closed vista is yet capable of infinite adaptation. The particular instance here shows the author's sketch for the development of the precinct of Liverpool cathedral, in which the vista is closed by the mass of the tower—but the scene is really given life by the great arch of the transept which is in black shade and swallows up the pedestrian's glance in mystery.

deflection

A variation on the closed vista is deflection, in which the object building is deflected away from the right angle, thus arousing the expectation that it is doing this to some purpose, i.e. that there is a place at the end of the street as yet unseen and of which this building forms a coherent part. This is invariably not so, but deflection arouses the thought.

projection and recession

This street in Rye demonstrates the charm of projection and recession. Instead of the eye taking in the street in a single glance, as it would in a street with perfectly straight façades, it is caught up in the intricacy of the meander and the result is a repose or dwelling of the mind which is wholly appropriate to the subject, which is a street of houses and not a fluid traffic route.

incident

The value of incident in a street— tower, belfry, silhouette feature, vivid colour and so on—is to entrap the eye so that it does not slide out into the beyond with resulting boredom. The skilful disposition of incident gives point to the basic shapes of the street or place; it is a nudge. The pattern is there but in the pre-occupation of life our attention must be drawn to it. I think that it is through the lack of incident that so many meticulously thought-out plans fail to come to life in three dimensions.

punctuation

If the vista seems like a complete sentence containing subject and predicate, the use of the word punctuation may clarify those demarcations of the enclosed phrase which this picture illustrates. In the continuing narrative of the street, function and pattern change from place to place; this should be acknowledged by some physical signal. The church, for instance, being a particular building, interrupts the alignment of the street and so closes one phrase and conceals the next, so that a pause is created.

narrows

The crowding together of buildings forms a pressure, an unavoidable nearness of detail, which is in direct contrast to the wide piazza, square or promenade, and by the use of such narrows it is possible to maintain enclosure without forbidding the passage of vehicles and pedestrians. In this way the articulation of the city into clear and well-defined parts is made more possible. In its own right narrowness has a definite effect on the pedestrian, inducing a sense of unaccustomed constriction and pressure.

fluctuation

In a town, a lived-in place, the lay-out of the spaces in which the public moves is a matter having a direct impact on the emotions, as has already been noted. To rationalize all these spaces into streets, and worse, a gridiron of streets, seems to deny the nature of people and extol a system which is fundamentally illogical because it is not derived from the character towns are known to possess. The typical town is not a pattern of streets but a *sequence of spaces* created by buildings. Fluctuation as shown here at Abingdon is implicit in this conception, it is the stimulation of our sense of position through moving from the wide to the narrow and out again into some fresh space.

undulation

Undulation is not just an aimless wiggly line; it is the compulsive departure from an unseen axis or norm, and its motive is delight in such proofs and essences of life as light and shade (the opposite of mono-chrome), or nearness and distance (the opposite of parallellism). It is like the rise and fall of foliage in the wind, like the same thought expressed in several different ways. Whatever form it may take it demonstrates the range of possibilities contained in one situation.

Fig. C.

closure

In enclosure the eye reacts to the fact of being completely surrounded. The reaction is static: once an enclosure is entered, the scene remains the same as you walk across it and out of it, where a new scene is suddenly revealed. Closure, on the other hand, is the creation of a break in the street which, whilst containing the eye, does not block out the sense of progression beyond as in the example at Buckingham. You'll probably get the hang of it by studying the siting of advertisements in the French village.

recession

The art of recession is present in the phenomenon, met with from time to time, of a scene which for some odd reason fails to fall into perspective. The laws of perspective may be immutable and it may be that the further away an object is the further away it seems to be. And yet unless we understand the art of recession it would not be wise to take this for granted. Examine, for instance, this view of Sheffield in which we see two buildings. Cover up each alternately with the hand and the impression is given that the dark building is much further away from us than the light modern building. This is due to the difference in scale between the two buildings and by manipulating scale one can obviously cause space to extend or diminish. (In the way that sculptured figures on buildings are often much smaller than life size in order to create the impression that the building is higher than it really is.) In the case of the Lake in St James's Park, below, the illusion of recession of water is created by hiding the actual end of the lake behind islands and we are left with a mystery instead of a plain fact.

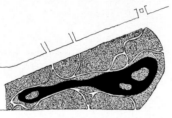

anticipation

We now turn to those aspects of here and there in which the here is known but the beyond is unknown, is infinite, mysterious, or is hidden inside a black maw.

First among these cases is anticipation. These two pictures clearly arouse one's curiosity as to what scene will meet our eyes upon reaching the end of the street.

infinity

There is a difference between sky and infinity. Sky is the stuff we see over the roof tops, as in the picture in Pimlico, below; infinity is a quite different thing. There are, I think, two ways in which the solitude and vastness of the sky can be made personal to us. Firstly, by the technique which served for truncation; by cutting out the middle distance and juxtaposing the immediate here with the sky, its more conventional overtones are somehow discarded and the deeper qualities aroused, as these two pictures, left, serve to remind us.

Secondly, we can consider the expected line of travel, the person's assessment of where he can walk. To substitute sky for road produces a shock which changes sky into infinity (see page 186).

mystery

From the matter-of-fact pavement of the busy world we glimpse the unknown, the mystery of a city where anything could happen or exist, the noble or the sordid, genius or lunacy. This is not Withenshawe.

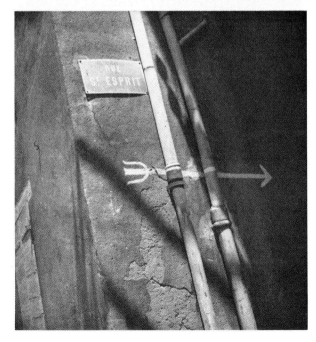

the maw

Black, motionless and silent, like a great animal with infinite patience, the maw observes nonchalant people passing to and fro in the sunlight. This is the unknown which utter blackness creates.

linking and joining: the floor

The last section of this part of the casebook is concerned with linking and joining, which have already been touched on in Netting. Today the environment is fragmented into separate pieces: separate houses, separate trees, separate zones like a series of totally unrelated notes played with one finger on a piano. The purpose of this book is to try to bring all the parts of the environment together into dramatic relationship so that the same notes are used but are arranged to form coherent chords and sequences. And whereas the whole of this book is in effect a series of examples of linking and joining, just here we are only considering the simplest forms, the floor, pedestrian ways and hazards.

Buildings, rich in texture and colour, stand on the floor. If the floor is a smooth and flat expanse of greyish tarmac then the buildings will remain separate because the floor fails to intrigue the eye in the same way that the buildings do. One of the most powerful agents for unifying and joining the town is the floor, as these two pictures so effectively demonstrate.

pedestrian ways

The pedestrian network links the town together in a viable pattern: it links place to place by steps, bridge and distinctive floor pattern, or by any means possible so long as continuity and access are maintained. The traffic routes sweep along impersonally but the tenacious and light-hearted pedestrian network creates the human town. Sometimes brash and extrovert, it may synchronize with the great traffic routes or with shops and offices, at other times it may be withdrawn and leafy; but it must be a connected whole.

continuity

The example opposite, from Shepton Mallet, shows in a very simple way how the open countryside and the town centre are directly linked together by a footpath. It should be read from left to right.

hazards

The process of linking and joining together raises the problem that although it may be visually rewarding to link here and there, it may not suit the immediate purposes of those who are charged with the control of the place to allow people or cattle to move about at will. Hence the use of hazards. Our diagram shows four kinds of hazards, the railing, water, planting and change of level. All these permit visual access whilst denying physical access. Perhaps the most well-known hazard is the ha-ha or concealed ditch which, from the viewing point of the squire's window, does not interrupt the green sweep of the landscape but excludes cattle from the home gardens. Below is an example from the Festival of Britain, showing how water is used to persuade people to pay for what they eat.

CONTENT

the categories

In this third section of the casebook we are concerned with the intrinsic quality of the various subdivisions of the environment, and start with the great landscape categories of metropolis, town, arcadia, park, industrial, arable and wild nature. These are the traditional categories and there is no certainty that they will continue to exist in the way we know them. On the other hand whatever the future may hold, one thing appears to be certain and that is the principle of categorization; for without distinction between one thing and another all we get is a form of porridge which will maintain life only if one can refrain from vomiting it up. At the present moment of change caused by individual transport and mass communications, the old pattern is breaking down. City centres are dying because they are too densely built for car access, the necessity for people to be in one place in order to do business and trade is lessening due to the various means of communication. Levelling of incomes is breaking up the large country estates, which are being exploited for housing the increased and ever more comfortably placed common man.

This explosion resembles nothing so much as a disturbed ant-hill with brightly enamelled ants moving rapidly in all directions, toot-toot, pip-pip, hooray.

From top to bottom:

METROPOLIS

TOWN

ARCADIA

The critical category is at the bottom: wild nature or hinterland. If there is plenty of this, the old ingrained laissez-faire form of expansion and exploitation causes little concern since the overall balance is still held. But once the hinterland is itself consumed then suddenly a new situation is created. All is thrown back on itself and the expansion of one category can only be achieved at the expense of another. In other words, free action comes to an end, and we are forced to regard the environment as a related complex of activities; just as the universal franchise forced politicians to regard society as a balance of relationships and not a system in which the privileged exploited the unwashed multitude. We, in England at least, are thus forced into developing the art of relationship in order to survive as a civilized country. Some of its benefits—and pitfalls—are shown in the next three pages.

Top to bottom:

PARK

INDUSTRY

ARABLE

WILD

the categorical landscape

A simple example of what I mean is this footpath, left, which follows the direction of the main road but is separated from it by a thick hedge. On the one side you have the roar and danger of lorries, on the other you have a secure and quite charming footpath commanding a pleasant view over the meadows. Thus, both motorist and pedestrian are better off. It is akin to the pedestrian network in the town. The vital clue in the situation is the hedge—the barrier—which serves to disengage the two functions. Now change the scale and move from the footpath to the great expanses of the landscape, as revealed in this air view of the Thames valley. If we compare the seventeenth and twentieth centuries, the most dramatic change is to be seen in the mobility of the individual. Instead of travel being itself laborious it is now a mere tediousness of getting on and off. The covering of distance is secondary to obtaining and vacating a seat. The old order achieved its typical pattern of compact cities and open country because of the tediousness of travel, which forced people to gravitate to centres. Today just the opposite obtains and people cannot leave each other fast enough. We appear to be forsaking nodal points for a thinly spread coast-to-coast continuity of people, food, power and entertainment; a universal wasteland. If everyone is leaping in different directions, then we simply turn the whole country into a chromium-plated chaos. But let us, for the sake of argument, postulate that a town shall have an edge and that at that edge the countryside shall begin. Is there any reason why this should not be so? Man is liberated in space and is able to overcome the problem of distance. That being so, a town can have an edge, for if the planner puts down an obstacle it simply means that at that point everyone suddenly starts leaping in the same direction; which turns chaos into an event. This is rather like creating huge hazards in order to bring clarity into the landscape. It is not zoning.

59

juxtaposition

This is a very rare example of the direct relationship between two categories, village and countryside. The unequivocal character of both is brought sharply together, there is no fluffing. On the one side the wind soughs through the trees and on the other the hollow tread of boots resounds on a stone pavement. Hollow is an appropriate word. The town turns in upon itself; it is enclosed and hollow in contrast to the exposure of nature. Below left is a scene in Coleshill which contains the same violence of contrast, this time between the pastoral and industrial. This scene is a typical categorical landscape but the smaller picture is not, it demonstrates the hopeless mixture of elements which turns all into a dull chaos.

immediacy

Preparation, softening up, railings, 'do be careful', and so on. Sometimes we get sick of all these conventions which get in between, which get in the way, and we long for the direct contact of immediacy, whether it be the edge of water or the edge of height. This quality of immediacy is implicit in what has been written before, the conception of categories and their juxtaposition to give drama and clarity to the landscape, and it is also germane to what now follows, the consideration of thisness or uniqueness.

thisness

Here and throughout the next fourteen pages we try to establish the idea of typicality, of a thing being itself. This wall of flint, for instance, has a typical texture and by white-washing it the pattern is given its most intense meaning as the sun illuminates it. We have only to compare this with the tarred section below to see the difference. On top the delight and assertion, below negation and indifference. The window of the string shop also displays this concentration and single-mindedness which seems to sum up the quality of string-ness. That character may be rich and very variously expressed —secrecy, entanglement, exposure, illusion, even absence—is the lesson to be learnt from this section.

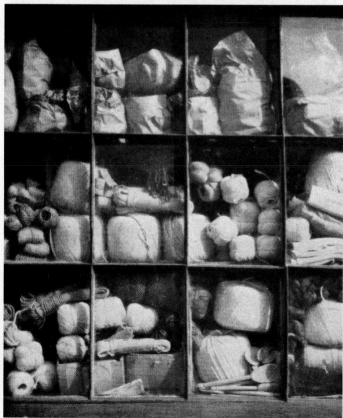

seeing in detail

By attention to detail, by training the eye to see in detail, the man-made world starts to grow in interest and quality. Small elements like this seem to have a life of their own. Walls, which to the quick glance have no significance, come to life upon more study. The example below, for instance, has been carefully and deliberately painted to bring out the quality of wall-ness. The errant meander of dots is simply an affirmation that the wall is alive, that it is a surface. In this sense the whole scene should gradually come to life.

secret town

These next few pages are devoted to the various kinds of quality to be seen in town and village. It is a very small selection and is only intended to stimulate the reader to discover and explore for himself.

Here in Birmingham two worlds exist side by side: the busy shopping and traffic route full of bustle, which is carried by the bridge over the canal, whose basin is silent and deserted, a secret town.

urbanity

Manchester Square sums up the whole character and quality of urban life, proportion, elegance, high density and the foil of a lush collective garden.

intricacy

This quality is perhaps the least understood (or the least demonstrated) in present day building, which seems to stop dead at the obvious, the slab block, the gridiron of curtain walling, the banality of pastel-shaded surfaces giggling down from the sky. But the quality of intricacy absorbs the eye. It is an extra dimension obtained through the knowledge and experience of true professionalism as opposed to the crudities of the amateur.

propriety

Propriety stems from the mutual respect which a true society should maintain amongst its members, which is not quite the same thing as manners. Our example is a somewhat astonishing shop fascia with lettering which might be thought out of place in a modest street, but since it is an example of the metalworker's craft it retains the sense of propriety. Propriety never seeks to stifle, rather is it self-expression within a civilized framework.

bluntness and vigour

In these two pictures we can sense a force which survives or bursts through the stylistic incompetence of the builder. Such buildings stand like rocks.

entanglement

Passing through the streets with their straight roof lines, flat walls and simple fenestration, suddenly the eye is caught up and entangled in a bunch of intricacy and wonder which is like a visual conundrum. The lamp-post at St Neots and the stagshorn seat in Somerset are long remembered, like burrs found on a jacket the week after a country walk.

nostalgia

The wind blows and the luxuriant creeper on the wall tosses and surges, but behind the glass in the dimly lit and silent room the solitary plant grows alone.

the white peacock

A haunted scene on Thames-side. Dull green foliage and the dead white of the wooden edging. Deserted. The opening leads only to an awareness of voices long since dead.

exposure

Emptiness, a great expanse of sky, geometry, these are some of the elements that create the feeling of exposure. The storms which have necessitated and shaped this construction recede so that we can walk with impunity, but this place really belongs to the sea.

intimacy

Luxuriant growth, enclosure, little sky and warm brickwork create the inward life of intimacy and cordiality. There is here a bright and blooming human vigour.

illusion

Up to now we have emphasized the categories and moods of the environment, the quality of thisness. The next phase is to bring together This and That to find out what emotions and dramatic situations can be liberated out of the various forms of relationship. The first example, illusion, is based on the bluff that This is That. We know that it is in the nature of water to be level in repose and yet, by cunningly ramping the retaining walls of the pool, retaining walls which, as everyone knows are always level, the illusion is created that the water is sloping. Levelness is sloping, This is That.

metaphor

Not quite so brazenly cheeky as illusion is the Metaphor which only hints that This is That, but there is great scope here for the power of suggestion. In the three examples shown on this opening the standard of suggestion and its aptness is not very penetrating, I'm afraid, but at least they convey the idea that the artillery shells surrounding a war memorial might have been bollards, that a huge circular structure when

thought of as the Colosseum might fit more easily into the mental climate of the 1900s, which put even gas holders into period costume, and that the Englishman's home, below, really is his castle. Crude as these examples are (and we could produce others even more banal) they yet contain a grain of guidance for the designer.

In preparation for the Festival of Britain I was asked to consider the treatment of Whitehall Court, a building which lay directly across the Thames from the main concourse of the exhibition. This building terminated in a great cluster of towers, flèches, gables and it was, in fact, a romantic, heraldic structure. The problem lay in making this interpretation obvious and clear to all, and this I attempted to do by erecting many flags and banners amongst the intricacy of the roof, picking them out with floodlights and leaving the bottom of the building in darkness so that the whole heraldic silhouette floated above the river at night.

the tell-tale

Certain objects possess the quality of being evocative and absolutely unmistakable. This boat, for instance, explains the region of which the particular view is only a part. The extension of this well-known fact in order to clarify or underline the character of different places could well be exploited further.

animism

Again the assertion, This is That, can be seen in examples of animism, the suggestion that a door is a face and, more directly, that a window is a mouth, can sometimes induce a sense of strangeness but can be very annoying when it occurs unwanted.

noticeable absence

In this category we include those effects in which the significant object is omitted, either in order to heighten its significance or because it is not really necessary and another thing can take over its function. In this example the wall of the church tower takes over the function of the cross which is, however, implicit in the situation. (Note that although it is implicit its absence has to some extent liberated the sculptor in his conception of the drama of Calvary.)

significant objects

Common objects often achieve distinction by reason of their self-contained force as sculpture or vivid colour and stand out in the general scene. The term is used more to describe those objects such as street furniture and structural features, which are not normally expected to attract the eye in this way, rather than designed works such as sculpture, posters, etc.

building as sculpture

From time to time buildings (which normally observe the conventions and fit into the landscape as architecture) emerge as another art, and to the extent that they do this they achieve a fresh significance due to the different standards to be applied. This lighthouse standing alone in the expanse of the shore has a Ben Nicholson base supporting interpenetrating volumes.

geometry

Geometry is akin to the foregoing. It is as though some influence descends out of the Newtonian order and vastness of the sky and imbues the landscape with its scale, detachment and austerity, rather as the appearance of the headmaster in a school classroom can change a chattering, restless and giggling group of jolly children into a serious and concentrating silence. The English landscape with its little trees and cosy hamlets is sometimes transmuted to a quite different character by the geometry which these pictures try to suggest.

multiple use

Or, to continue the interplay, This and That can co-exist. Ever since people got really serious about planning one of the main endeavours has been to put people into sunny, healthy homes away from dirty, smelly and noisy industry. Whilst no one will seriously quarrel with this, the principle of segregation and zoning goes marching on, with the result that we are in danger of losing the great unities of social living. The West End gets more and more offices to the exclusion of theatres and

houses, vast armies of people commute, people object to having a church or a pub built in their street because of the noise. Some magistrates even say you are breaking the law if you stand still on a pavement. But true living accepts the joys of togetherness along with the setbacks. On balance it is worth it. The scene at Bankside on the Thames as it might be developed with residential development amongst the warehouses is a typical multiple use view, whilst below, the whole attitude is summed up in the French illustrations, in which the ground is regarded as belonging to all: to the players of boules and also to the train when it wants it.

foils

The last section of this casebook is
devoted to the consideration that in
the complex world already outlined,
with its varying categories, its differing kinds of character, its buildings
of diverse styles and materials, the
relation of these separate entities
could result in the creation of urban
drama. For just as the interaction of
Here and There produced a form of
emotional tension, so the relationship
of This and That will produce its
own form of drama which will exist
inside the overall spatial framework.
This marriage of opposites, illustrated
in the next nine pages, may be a
matter of scale, distortion, tree
planting or publicity, but it succeeds because This is good for That.

In Bath within the framework of
the enclosure Victorian, Classical and
Gothic buildings are grouped together and produce a scene as natural
and comfortable as a clubroom.
Below in Oxford the monumental
Clarendon building shares the street
with purely modest domestic buildings. We are perhaps too well used
to this kind of effect in England but
if you cover first one half of the
scene with your hand and then the
other half, something of the surprise
of the situation will emerge.

relationship

This example in the City of London shows the kind of flowing rhythm that can be created between buildings, the accidental repetition of angles in pediment, flying shore and stairway which fixes a typical pattern for a fleeting second. Below right, is shown the exact opposite of all this, the total segregation of one building from its surroundings. It isn't so much the separation of the building by distance which offends, it is the barrier of encircling road which really tells, for if some of the houses fronted on to the main grassy expanse the connection would have been made and a feeling of community created. By contrast the integration of an ancient monument into the structure of today is happily shown in the example from Canterbury, below left.

scale

The quality of scale in buildings, constructions and trees is one of the most potent tools in the art of juxtaposition, and reference has already been made to it in the case of recession. Scale is not size, it is the inherent claim to size that the construction makes to the eye. By and large the two go hand in hand, a big building does have a big scale and a small building a small scale. It is in the manipulation of the borderline that the designer's skill is called for. (In the case of the office building, below right, we see how a big building is made to seem vaster by the extravagance of scale.) The first illustration, left, shows the juxtaposition of two quite different scales, the robust scale of the ashlar wall and the equally assertive but modest scale of the hut. This just about sums it up. Both wall and hut have their own scales intensified by being seen together, the big is bigger and the small smaller. A similar situation arises in the drawing below of the proposals for Liverpool Cathedral precinct where the domestic and the monumental are juxtaposed.

scale on plan

Of special interest to the planner is the sense of scale in the question of town layout. The case quoted here by Ebbe Sadolin (*A Wanderer in London*. Methuen) is, to my mind, of extreme importance to all in charge of new layouts. His own words and drawing: 'The little park is just by the Thames between Chelsea Embankment and Cheyne Walk. It is a delightful place with lovely old trees, shrubs, rock garden, seats, statues of famous men and an unobstructed view of an old pub called "The King's Head and Eight Bells". In short, it is well worth a visit. You can enjoy the green leaves and rest for a while in the pleasant company of the people of Chelsea. But when you try to find it on the map you begin to wonder. For where exactly is this park in your otherwise reliable atlas of London, which is a large-scale affair in a bulky tome of 131 pages? It must be there for here is the bridge, here is the embankment, and here—yes, there it is, that little object the size of a very small pine-needle, down in the left-hand corner under the word "Walk". That is the entire park.'

Prairie planners please note.

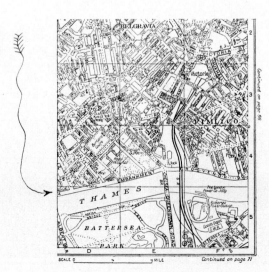

Continued on page 95

Continued on page 71

distortion

By deliberately distorting the scale
by giantism a shock is produced as
of some sudden violence of nature or
of unreality, whereas distortion by
reduction produces the effect of a
jewel-box.

trees incorporated

Of all the natural aids to townscape the tree is surely the most ubiquitous, and the relationship between trees and towns has a long and honourable history. The conception that trees were structures in just the same way as buildings led to pleaching and an architectural layout of planting, but today the tree is more usually accepted in its own right as a living organism which is pleased to dwell amongst us. In this way new relationships are possible between our own organic architecture and the natural structure. The first example shows the volume created by the clump of trees: we all know the meaning of this, the sense of enclosure and space, a space that can be entered and left. Here the house is situated inside this space with the result that a structural volume is created akin to the classical portico, left.

The parallel of foliage and tracery in this Spanish scene, below, produces a momentary and transient synchronization which asserts a community of interest beyond the normal and is to that extent remarkable. There is a whole field of study of the textures and habits of growth of trees which can be exploited. For just as trees have different characteristics, fastigiate or drooping, geometric or fluffy, polished or velvet, so these qualities may be used in dramatic conjunction with buildings, either to extend the conception or to offset it as a foil.

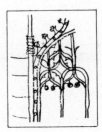

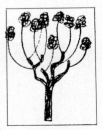

In this Swedish example trees have been used as a sort of living wallpaper to decorate the vast geometry of the grain silos.

The last example, and the most homely, shows the exterior decorator at work. The tree has been placed in the village centre in just the same way that a bowl of flowers is placed on the living-room table, and for the same reason, because it is green and fresh and a foil to the permanent structure.

calligraphy

One of the most rewarding pastimes is to take a really incisive writing instrument and draw on white paper or walls. In these two balconies at Cheltenham the slender and cursive ironwork is drawn on to the simple white walls creating a most precise and delicate foil, whilst the more sturdy serpent of the seat slides into supporting position like a satire on the rough utilitarianism of the boards.

publicity

Publicity raises the temperature in the world of planning because there are two things concerned, first the question of propriety and second the vitality of the medium in the urban scene. To those who hold architecture to be sacred our first illustration is anathema. In fact, since advertising is accepted as a part of our society then the actual morals of the case don't enter the argument; it is all taken for granted and we are left with a house of lettering which has its own charm and vitality as a foil to the street. Below, in the view of the city centre, we hint at the kind of night-time development (Piccadilly Circus, Times Square) which has a surrealist drama of shapes, lights and move-ment in which the message sinks back under the free show, the evening-out sensation. Architecture? We could do without it and have a neat framework for the variations of publicity.

taming with tact

—or the intrusion of man into the wilderness without vulgarity. Of special interest today when the wild places of our countryside are being invaded by the constructions of man are these pictures which may help to underline the delicacy of the situation. Our picture of the cliffs at Corsica is remarkable for the reason that the houses enter into the spirit, into the wildness of the scene by crowding up to the edge of the cliff, up to the danger point. Had they been set back a hundred feet or so all would have been lost and ruined since the effect would then have been one of a prissy suburbanism (which is precisely what is wrong with some of the nuclear power stations that are being built in the wildest parts of this country).

A reminder to civic gardeners is contained in the picture of a seat at Bidston Hill, which carries with it no hint that the land is occupied or municipally digested. Here is a seat which might have been left by a traveller.

The fourth and last section of the casebook concerns itself not with the various moves in the game but with the intrinsic quality of things made—structures, bridges, paving, lettering and trim—which create the environment.

How to describe what is meant? Imagine yourself in a London pub which closes for the night at 11 p.m. The landlord calls 'last orders' and later calls 'time'. At this moment he might be seen to take the dishcloth with which he has been drying the pots and hang it up over the beer pulls. This simple action is in the Functional Tradition, it is unequivocal, pithy and wonderfully economical. To put a notice on the counter saying 'sorry, too late' is part of the bumbling, fluffy and muddle-headed tradition. The Functional Tradition has something of peasant cunning to it.

structures

What is intrinsic to the problem is allowed to speak for itself instead of being overlaid with an alien formalism. The Thames bridge contains a wholly convincing relationship of angles and the significant metal plates are picked out in black. Workshops like the one to the left have been built since the eighteenth century and this proves the validity of the tradition. A comparison with the awkward and heavy bridge above serves to underline the pithy and taut quality of the tradition.

railings

Railings are first and foremost placed in positions of potential danger as a visual warning, and only secondly as a physical barrier; the very simplest means will suffice to give this warning. The iron rail on this footbridge only occurs where the continuity of the bank reaches outwards and is a minimum structure. The metal rails, below left are delicate lines drawn at danger points and not ponderous and stuffy barriers, like those shown below, which are right outside the tradition.

fences

The function of a fence is to enclose property, to exclude unwanted people and animals. The picket fence is perhaps the oldest and yet still the most effective form of fence with its pointed tops and trim effect of black and white. Below left is a composite barrier which consists of heavy stone bollards, enough to serve as a warning to traffic, connected by light chains which warn the unthinking pedestrian. These are direct and practical steps taken to avoid disaster, unlike the pompous and 'designed' bridge rail below.

steps

To men who have been out fishing in half a gale these steps probably seem like a haven of safety. At any rate, in their context, they give a penetrating insight into the quality we are trying to isolate. The two illustrations at the foot of the page are of the same construction in which the direct, left, and the superfluous, right, are shown side by side (see also taming with tact).

black and white

The embellishment of structures usually takes the form of painting with black and white, a process which often performs a function in itself as well as creating a trim effect. This is especially so in positions where security is of paramount importance such as in harbours and on the road. This detail of the harbour at Lyme Regis shows the use of white walls which are like a signal.

The sheer vivacity and gaiety of black and white is well demonstrated in the little beach hut at the bottom. The two rough squares of whitewash on the field wall are a signal, and the imposition of geometry, however crudely, makes the point that this is here by design and not by accident.

texture

Far too often in recent years the progressive architect's attention has been directed to the big idea, the town plan, the national plan, the cosmic plan, to the exclusion of more local and particular interests. The result has been that he has begun to lose his ability to see other than with the mind's eye. In many ways he is like a child who, after an earlier period of uninhibited pleasure in simple visual experience, finds his interest in seeing atrophied by his preoccupation with learning (that is, his growing intellectual development), with disastrous effect on his creative faculties. The burden of technical awareness hangs heavily on the practising architect, and the sense of social responsibility often assumes the proportion and character of an incubus as well as a stimulant. A wholly satisfying and virile architecture cannot flourish unless in its practice social justification is lavishly compounded with personal pleasure, a wholesome delight in the creative process itself as well as an appreciation of the end in view. There is no need to regard such naive delight as almost sinful, since

without the ingredient of sensuous enjoyment the practice of architecture must inevitably degenerate into little more than a sordid routine, or at the most the exercise of mere intellectual cleverness. In this light, the examples of texture here can be gladly accepted as a stimulation to be found in the ordinary scene.

lettering

Since the day when the town-crier no longer needed to shout himself hoarse, but could paste up a notice that most people were able to read, display types have never ceased to multiply in quantity and variety. Practically every yard of townscape has its house-name, placard, road-sign, fascia board, advertising hoarding, bus-route sign or road name. The truly functional type-face is the one that, properly spaced, makes its message clear from the distance at which it is intended to be read. It may be bold, black and purposeful, or alternatively bold and white on a black ground. It may be trim, slim and well-formed when its message is secondary to the bolder one. Many of the early nineteenth-century play-bills bristle with such type-faces and have never been improved upon. They provide much better models for imitation than most of the modern display types produced today, and

there is an immense variety still available, and still used by auctioneers, canal authorities and jobbing printers. In comparison to the selection of sturdy and virile type-faces shown we contrast the opposite. Sans serif of the type shown below—all too commonly used—is functionalism without feeling, it is completely characterless and totally lacks the robustness of the example on the previous page. The shop lettering, bottom, debilitated and deformed, overlooks the prime need for legibility.

trim

The smallest details of the street or civic space should fit into the townscape in performing their individual functions. The circular seat and the corrugated edging are representative of the vast complexity of detail met with in civic gardens and squares that are frequently called ornamental. These two are selected for the satisfactory way in which they avoid such a description, yet achieve in their functional way, embellishment of a far higher quality. Of the many small structures to be found this public lavatory may sum up the functional vigour of expression. The two examples below show what happens when this clarity of purpose becomes obscured.

the road

Road signs must be clear and make their message at a glance. White letters painted on the road do not obstruct, and they site their messages in the spot most easy to see. In this satisfactory way the road takes over the nautical black and white. Bollards,

traffic-signs and lamp-posts are the repetitive vertical elements of the street scene. Their large number puts a premium on simplicity and clarity, which is clearly the reason why street symbols have borrowed freely from the nautical tradition of black and white. It should not be difficult to sort out the wheat from the chaff (above and below, for example) on this page.

the private square: enclosed

GENERAL STUDIES: Squares for All Tastes

Town squares, once the preserve of privilege, have since the wartime salvage of railings become public spaces. (This is taken from a study written in 1947.) It is unlikely and undesirable that they should all return to their old use, but so far no definite proposals have been put forward for bringing them into line with the needs of a changed society. These pages demonstrate, with examples chosen from London, how Britain's squares could be made to serve life as it is lived in our towns today. The particular squares named are token ones merely used for the purposes of illustration. The aim is to put forward principles which may be applied anywhere. Right at the start let it be pointed out that where function and architectural unity still march together no change is advocated.

Thus where the square is still residential it could

97

the private square: open

well remain a private or communal garden, enclosed and screened from passers-by by the usual railings.

A variation on the private enclosed square is the private open square, which is guarded only by hazards such as those of judicious planting and changes of level. In quiet neighbourhoods such squares do not need further protection, and this immunity encourages a freer excursion into urban landscaping in the technical meaning of informal non-academic layout.

With justification we may assume the precinctual organization of cities and a more equal distribution of privileges. Put together in terms of town planning, the result will be the square as quadrangle protected from all but local traffic.

While the metropolitan square is an amenity which should not remain barred to all but the few who happen to overlook it, that does not imply the obliteration of all distinctions. As Mayfair happens to be expensive and exclusive, then this should determine the character of Grosvenor Square in its renascent public form. The presence of the American Embassy, together with the square's wartime associations as moral G.H.Q. of American troops in England, has prompted the authorities to make of it a memorial to President Roosevelt, a scheme which has had wide public support. Why not make Grosvenor Square a real American Corner? Not the America associated in the eyes of Europeans with vulgarization; the connection is with Fifth Avenue rather than Broadway. The best American food, exclusive underground cinema, swans and fountains (but not a soda fountain). On great occasions the American Embassy could hold garden parties in the square. A corner of London that is America for both Londoners and Americans.

the public square

A view of Leicester Square in the eighteenth century would be virtually impossible to reconcile with its present condition, a boisterous jungle of traffic, changing signs, vivid lettering and garish posters. The desperate pre-war attempt to preserve a be-railed garden, although a pleasing evidence of official grit and determination, was always a flop. It simply induced a depressing feeling of prohibition, the feeling that one was being inhibited for the wrong reason. Far better to obtain the feeling of space and openness by sweeping away the railings and laying down a paved floor throughout. There are sufficient cafés round the square to rent space for tables, as is done in France, and gaily coloured velariums suspended between the trees would give protection from birds and rain. What is most important, however, is for the landscapist to understand the vital and popular visual appeal of the Leicester Square type of landscape. The fact that it is the aesthetic expression of the dive and pin-table saloon, is no reason for the urban planner to turn up his nose. These activities, for better or for worse, are a part of urban life, and as such make a very valuable contribution to the visual scene.

the popular square

the square as quadrangle: municipal square

In a complete squares policy there should be a place for everything—even the undiluted monumental. The existing buildings and proposals for the future of Russell Square suggest that its character should be municipal and monumental. The buildings which surround it are on the whole massive and monumental, London University, the Imperial and Russell Hotels and the new office blocks. Where there is a marked change in the use and character of the boundaries of the square it is reasonable to suggest a general change of character to utilize the drama which traffic in volume can produce. That is to say, the monumentality should flow right through with all its devices of the axis, fountains, seats and sculpture, and so produce an unsubtle yet impressive effect of metropolitanism.

the square as quadrangle: the collegiate square

With the reorganization of traffic and the formation of precincts the flow of vehicles will be reduced to those which have business in the area. Even so in certain squares there should be pedestrian priority—that is to say, if there is a pedestrian and a taxi, the taxi gets out of the way of the pedestrian. The attempt to preserve a few square feet of cat-ridden, sooty turf in the smaller public squares is surely hardly worth the trouble. Rather pave the whole area as in the Temple Courts, which will emphasize the collegiate atmosphere and the pedestrian priority; it will also emphasize the fact that these squares have become the property of all. The quadrangle is the basis or neutral pattern which will vary as local conditions change. It may be municipal as in the example of Russell Square, exclusive as in Grosvenor Square, popular as in Leicester Square, or quietly collegiate as in this example of Manchester Square.

Cross as Focal Point

The idea of the town as a place of assembly, of social intercourse, of meeting, was taken for granted throughout the whole of human civilization up to the twentieth century. You might assemble in the Forum at Pompeii or round the market cross, but you still assembled; it was a ritual proper to man, both a rite and a right. Nor in the general way did you have to explain whether your motives were proper or profane. Men are gregarious and expect to meet. In all ages but ours, that is. Here the Poultry Cross at Salisbury 2, and over page, is taken as an example of the sort of process that endangers places of congregation in our age.

Observation suggests that a fixed object acts as a magnet to movable objects: in 1, at Minehead, Somerset, the trees have attracted to themselves a weighing machine and a nameplate device. It is obvious that the motive for this arrangement arises from the desire to be tidy and not clutter up free space with separate objects over which people could stumble.

1

2

3

4

However, the most movable object in town is the human being and, for possibly different reasons, he too needs anchorage. He needs it in the various outdoor activities of trade, recreation and social life. Now, to provide open space so that these activities can take place at all, is in itself not really sufficient. Open space as an element in the town is essential but it needs also to be furnished with such objects as will turn the disassociated stream of people into groups as in 3, previous page, at Orvieta, Italy. For people are gregarious and need the incident, the feature or the anchor. In the case of a tree one might say that it provides shade or shelter and of the covered market cross—the same thing. Yet the anchor provides a little more than the purely utilitarian attraction. By construction it is im-

The Poultry Cross is a handsome structure, it is also of considerable age and given these two qualities then the happy partnership between planet and satellite, between anchor and people, stands in great danger. The process is as follows: more and more traffic is forced through the streets and open space is coveted by the engineers. In search of this they espy the Poultry Cross, 5, with its surrounding pavement, a valuable piece of ground. The only thing that preserves the open space from immediate seizure is the obstinate cross. However, it is discovered to be a work of architecture and should be protected, it is railed in, 6, and the traffic edges closer. Divorced now from its function it only awaits the final retirement to a country park whilst in the town the stream of people circulates, the traffic moves faster and another slice of the pedestrian town is washed away, 7, another anchor is lost to another open space. Fortunately this has not yet happened in Salisbury, but it may not be long.

5

6

7

movable and hence, by use, it becomes a recognized rallying point.

The Poultry Cross in Salisbury illustrates this last point since, as can be seen in 4, the market stalls erected in its shade have their own tarpaulin covers and do not rely on the structure for protection against the elements. Rather do they rely on its immovability, its security in the surging tide of traffic and shoppers.

Closure

Closure, as indicated on p. 47, may be differentiated from Enclosure, p. 25, by contrasting 'travel' with 'arrival'. Closure is the cutting up of the linear town system (streets, passages, etc.) into visually digestible and coherent amounts whilst retaining the sense of progression. Enclosure on the other hand provides a complete private world which is inward looking, static and self-sufficient.

Hence closure is not intended to mean the closing of a vista, such as Buckingham Palace at the end of the Mall. For here the sense of progression and continuity is lacking whilst closure is rather the articulation of movement (the closed vista falls into the camp of enclosure). A building or wall which creates closure will generally provide also a feeling of anticipation.

Closure is effected by some irregularity or asymmetry of layout whereby the path from source to goal is not automatically and inevitably revealed to the eye as in the gridiron plan. This irregularity divides the route into a series of recognizable visual statements, each one effectively and sometimes surprisingly linked to the other, so that progress on foot is rendered interesting by reason of

the subdivisions created, which are human in scale
the provision of incident
the sense of unrolling or revealing
identification

Gloucester

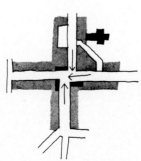

Chester

A simple example of 'identification' can be obtained by comparing the centres of Gloucester and Chester, both similar in plan, left. In Gloucester the two main roads cross cleanly at right angles with the result that the visitor is confused, he cannot get his bearings since the crossing looks the same from every approach. At Chester, on the other hand, the crossing is staggered slightly so that buildings block the view and clarify the situation by the provision of landmarks.

This in itself is justification enough for departing from the 'logical' straight line layout but it might also be noted that the building making a closure is in a key position and consequently such a position might be allocated to buildings which generally accentuate the towniness of towns—town hall, church, hotel, big store, etc., etc.

The photograph, above, a typical village scene (East Chiltington), shows the application of closure. The projecting house effectively contains the eye as the road sweeps past. Yet how often is the art in such a device taken for granted?

It is only when it is compared with cases where no art is used such as the obvious one of dead conformity to the road, above, that we realize the difference between closure and mere change of direction.

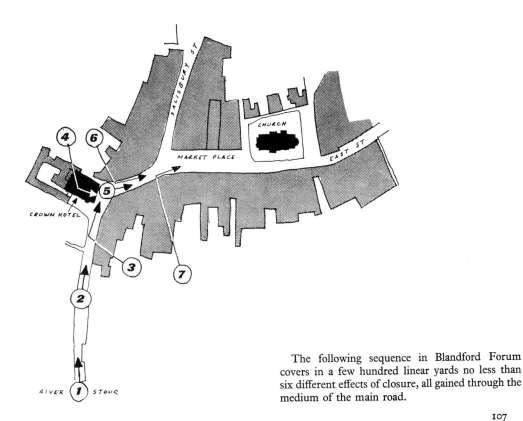

The following sequence in Blandford Forum covers in a few hundred linear yards no less than six different effects of closure, all gained through the medium of the main road.

1 The square solid mass of the Crown Hotel faces the approach road as it crosses the river Stour. And what we see is not a secondary elevation, as might be expected, but the main elevation. Here is exactly the kind of entrance a market town ought to have, a pub which by blocking the vista both invites you in and fills you with anticipation as to what's just around the corner. The narrow gap . . .

2 . . . opens out as the road drives to the centre and the vista is cut short by the deflection of the road to the right. Closure transforms a line into an area, a road into a place, square or quad.

3 A quad, however, which is not only human in scale and not stuff-shirt, but also not static. The quad proper creates static enclosure, the effect of which is to make the observers want to settle down if only on a seat; closure also creates enclosure but of the roving kind under which the eye (and the body) is forced forward from the one before to the one after. As the next materializes, the last disintegrates.

4 As one turns round the town begins to be revealed; not all at once but coherently. (The letter A is a recognition point for the next picture below. Here the next theme is introduced in the shape of a new piece of stage scenery coming in at an angle.)

5 And now there is a clear example of the quad-like structure or sequence that is possible by the use of closure. The sudden widening and oblique angle of the road produce the sense of area rather than line, and the eye is made conscious of arrival by the sudden appearance of the town hall. In fact, however, there is no square. These are street scenes pure and simple.

6 And as the scene unfolds, the church tower, the climax, is at last revealed. Due to the angle of the road it performs the last act of closure before . . .

7 . . . we enter the wide main street where everything is revealed. This is the finale to the successive acts of closure which formed a series of dramatic visual events in a co-ordinated sequence which provides, on a delightful domestic scale, a model piece of townscape. Accidental or deliberate? Those who invariably answer accidental to that question might like to be reminded that the Bastard brothers, architects, rebuilt the town complete after a fire in the eighteenth century.

The Line of Life

The essential function of a town should be visible from a single glance at the plan. This obviously is because the arrangement of its parts reflects certain lines of force which represent also the combination of circumstances that brought the town into being. Conversely, when a town lacks character and structure, the failure can nearly always be traced to some impediment in the relationship of form to function, whereby the lines of force have become confused, or have disappeared. This explains the amorphous character of so many modern towns, but it also suggests the planner's opportunity. Since his task, in any case, is one of resolving conflicts and allocating the regard to be paid to rival demands, and since the procedure he follows is inevitably one of particularization, the success with which he discovers and gives visual interpretation to the most significant lines of force will largely determine whether the town achieves an intelligible and *characteristic* form.

This opportunity is best revealed in a town—such as the typical seaside town—where the lines of force have an obvious and immediate relationship with lines of demarcation in the geographical sense. The very *raison d'être* of the seaside town is the line along which land and water meet, and that perhaps explains why character survives better in the seaside town than elsewhere. On the following pages three towns on the south coast of England are used as a demonstration of the sort of action a planner, aware

of the significance of this relationship, might take in trying to preserve or create a good urban character.

We start with Brixham, a place where the meeting of land and sea forms a natural amphitheatre enclosing the harbour, and the shape of the town can hardly do otherwise than coincide with the one dominating line of force—in this case the gathering of a community protectively round the shipping to which it owes its living. In this lies Brixham's character, a character that is already clearly and vigorously expressed. All the planner has to do is to intensify the result visually, so that every particle of drama and logic can be wrung from it.

In the next example, Fowey, the line of force has still one dominating character, the crowding activity along the waterfront, but here, with houses and cliffs descending straight into the water and the absence of a continuous quay, a barrier is placed between the inhabitant and what is, in fact, the real line of force, the coast-line. Steps occasionally run down to it from the interior, but there is no continuous access along it. All that is needed is to link these points together and the real character of Fowey falls into line.

Looe is a more complex case, where several lines of force operate simultaneously, and the planner's task is to disentangle them and allow each its proper topographical expression, building up the town's character by this means.

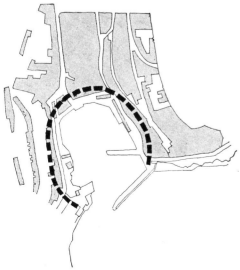

Brixham

As good an illustration as you could wish for of the liveliness of scene and character that ensues when the natural lines of force, deriving from a town's origin and function, find an immediate echo in its topography. The harbour (facing page) is the effective centre of the town, which is built up into terraces round the almost enclosed inner harbour in the form of a natural amphitheatre. It is a combined social and working

centre; visitors promenade the quays and treat the fish market as a free entertainment; coloured sails and flags and the whirling wings of seagulls combine to create a stimulating effect—that of a busy industrial scene permanently *en fête*.

In these circumstances nothing is required of the planner but a watchful eye to make sure the present compact unbroken line of surrounding buildings is not interfered with—his only additional task being to provide car parks out of sight of the harbour, so that the sparkling water-front scene is no longer blocked by the dark shapes of rows of parked cars. The planner can, however, intensify the existing character of the amphitheatre of buildings by seeing they are given the maximum visual coherence. An obvious way of doing this is to whitewash them. At present the buildings surrounding Brixham harbour are mostly a mixture of duns and greys (previous page). The unifying effect of whitewash is shown in the picture above.

as it is

Fowey

As with Brixham, Fowey's topographical shape reflects pretty closely the *raison d'être* of the town: a built-up line where land and water meet. But here, instead of a circle of buildings round an enclosed harbour it takes the form of a line of buildings along the shore of an estuary. Brixham has the special virtue, from which it derives much of its vitality, that the line where land and water meet is a social as well as an architectural line—the line where sailors and landsmen freely mingle. Fowey, on the other hand, has the failing that the satisfactorily built-up line of architecture acts as a barrier, only allowing human contact with the water at one or two isolated points.

The planner's first task then is to arrange some sort of continuous access, so as to revitalize the water-line—see proposals on the following pages. The principle he should follow is that a mere physical line along the waterfront (such as the cliff-top roadway bounded by a wall in the picture above) is not enough; there must instead be intimate living contacts all along the line, below.

as it might be

115

as it is

The water-front architecture of Fowey plunges, logically and dramatically, straight into the estuary; in many cases sea-wall and house-wall are one. But only at certain points is there public access to the water, with the result that Fowey loses the opportunity of drawing maximum vitality and character from the fact of the fullest social life being lived along the line where land and water meet.

The planner's object must be to provide excitement all along the front without destroying its architectural continuity. One way of achieving this would be to build a pedestrian walk at whatever changing levels the topography suggests, linking up the existing access points into a continuous line. The pictures show how this walk might appear at various points where access is now unobtainable. Such a walk would be completely in keeping with Fowey's present intricately built-up pedestrian character.

Looe

A more complex case than Brixham or Fowey, because the line is a branching one, eventually becoming two lines, one along the river, one at right angles facing the open sea (plan opposite). Each stretch of water-front has its own individuality, expressing the fact that the most intense social life is lived along two fronts, each different in character but to which Looe jointly owes its existence.

as it might be

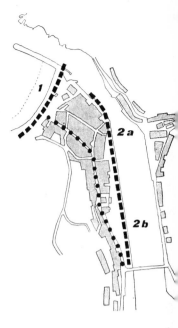

The sea-front line is a plage (top and 1) sheltered on one side by a pier, on the other by the rocky headland of the bay. The river-front line is a fish market (bottom and 2a) similar in style to that at Brixham. The unsatisfactory part of Looe is that stretch of the line before it divides, 2b—before the High Street branches off from the river-front and leads away to the plage. This is where the linear water-front character should be most strongly marked, where the inhabitants should have most opportunity of living a water-front life—both spiritually and physically. But in fact the line here has disintegrated, leaving a directionless no-man's-land, used by the council for parking cars.

What is called for is a boulevard where shops —this is an extension of the main shopping street— forming a continuous base to the cliff that rises above, could face a wide promenade, where the inhabitants could stroll beneath trees, conscious of partaking in the life of the river.

The drawing opposite suggests how this key stretch of Looe could be brought back into character by providing a car park elsewhere and allowing the boulevard its rightful use as a meeting place of fisherfolk and landlubbers. Under the trees fish stalls and restaurants overlook the water near the fish market.

A moral tale. Top: the idyllic river scenery just above Looe; thick woods climb down to the water's edge. Second: the town itself—at the same time a river and a seaside town, but in either case as compactly built up as a town of this character should be. The river-front is lined with houses in continuous terraces; the sea-front the same. Third: the linear principle abandoned; nearby headlands ruined by isolated buildings: their bad example is affecting Looe itself; on the hills behind the town the terrace formation has been allowed to disintegrate, destroying the emphasis on the line from which Looe, obeying the magnetic attraction of the water-front, derives its whole character.

Legs and Wheels

The street scene is bounded by sky, walls and road. The sky, ever changing, the walls, old and crumbling or sharp and new; variety of style and contour, texture, colour and character. The floor—a monotone of tarmac.

Headed by the fire engine and ambulance, the motor-car has penetrated every crack and crevice of our cities, lanes, yards and courts. All the richness and variety of the floor has been submerged in the traffic flood and inhabitants of buildings venture out at their peril, making their way by means of islands, refuges, safety zones and beacons.

When we consider that in the normal urban block streets occupy about one-third of the total area we get some idea of the loss which this mechanized age is sustaining. Instead of walls and floor being in harmony, the floor linking or separating architectural elements and expressing the kind of space which exists between buildings, it is as though the buildings were models plonked down on a blackboard.

There are many materials which can be used to revitalize the town's floor, to reinforce the highway code and, by indicating different uses, in time to establish conventional behaviour—flagstones for pedestrians only, cobbles, setts, slate tiles, mosaic, gravel, grass. They can be light or dark, rough or smooth, plain or intricate. The possibilities of design are immense. Yet today they are all sacrificed to the technical necessities of the contact between the floor and a rubber tyre.

Traffic inside a building is mainly pedestrian, collisions are rare and fatalities even rarer. In the forecourt or drive, in the open air, things are still sane and reasonable. The odd car realizes its intrusion and makes way for the pedestrian. But as the pedestrian's world dwindles to thin ribbons of pavement on either side of the traffic stream—let him beware. The warm, comforting security of indoors passes too quickly to the exposure of the hunted.

Thus we have two results arising from the universal flooding of our towns by the motor-car: (*a*) the suppression of variety and character in the ground surface; (*b*) the invasion of the pedestrian reserves.

Point (*a*), however, is by no means implicit in the existence of motor traffic, since if the business of organizing road traffic efficiently were studied, a solution might be found in the use of road surfaces to indicate the road's use for a particular purpose. A coloured pencil is more easily chosen out of its box if the outside of the pencil is coloured to match the lead instead of the colour being named. In the same way a universal convention of colours and patterns indicating such things as one-way streets, parking, pedestrian crossings and so on would allow the road to be read at a glance. This would, as a result, introduce a new functional aesthetic into the urban view.

First of all, a system of priorities to stem and direct the flood of traffic. Secondly, a set of road conventions to enforce this, such conventions being integral with the road itself and of such a nature as to enhance the surrounding buildings.

For example, a street or square limited to pedestrian use would be protected by a stretch of cobbles across its access. *Convention:* no car may drive across cobbles. The drawings opposite and on the next page illustrate the point.

pedestrians only

There are occasions when absolute pedestrian priority is desirable. This may occur in the case of cathedral precincts, and such special cases as schools, squares and old people's houses. Nevertheless, entrance for fire engines and ambulances is essential, and this precludes the use of any physical barrier. The illustration shows a suitable convention—a stretch of cobbles across the access road through which a flagged walk provides pedestrian access (since cobbles are difficult to walk on). Cobbles are regarded as an alternative to grass. Inside this protecting band the designer is free to employ any material in any pattern. *Convention:* for car-drivers cobbles mean NO ENTRY.

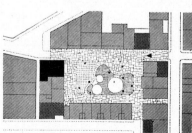

pedestrian priority

No one denies the place of swiftly moving traffic in the life of a town. It is the universal spread of traffic, its arrogant seizure of *all* roads, that calls for protest. It is very human to want to drive right up to one's front door, but in admitting this we also admit the possibility of admitting any traffic. In this way a street which may have a dozen cars belonging to it is, as often as not, busy all day with traffic which uses it as a short cut or an easy way round a major cross-roads. This example (the viewpoint is shown by the arrow on the plan) shows the street or square in which traffic is limited to that having business in the area.

There are two points to notice here: (*a*) The scarcity of traffic will have the effect of enhancing the domestic character of the whole square. (*b*) Those motorists who do enter it, being on their own ground, will observe the nicety of good manners and regard for others which is so difficult to observe when one is on 'foreign' terri-tory, i.e. when we do not fear recognition and do as we please. *Convention:* the area to be paved with flag-stones means *pedestrian priority.* Demarcation of pavement, if any, is left to discretion of designer. In this drawing a two-foot band of setts is used with bollards at intervals.

Hazards

Materials of the visual planner are lumps of rock, cement, wood, earth, metal, tar, grass, in various states, tended or otherwise, and hills, water, people, the stuff of which the world is made. His urban job is so to dispose and relate these lumps of matter as to create out of the demands of the human race for shelter and communication, leisure and ceremonial, a humane kind of urban scenery: a humanized townscape. Although many of his problems may be large ones dealing with such matters as the siting of traffic arteries, their realization depends on mere nuances of design, a truth which perhaps amongst visual planners only architects perceive in all its meaning. Selected here in illustration of this truth is a problem described as the problem of the HAZARD, a problem dismissed by most planners as a mere matter of fencing, hedge or railing, wire or yew. Thus regarded the problem seems simple, but as realized in our cities the insensitive borough engineer's methods of enclosure are the most common and most fruitful sources of

visual crime. One of the war's advantages was that the removal of many kinds of not strictly essential fencing had something of the effect of the removal of restrictions; they opened out prospects of a more freely flowing world. Today as the restrictions pile up again the authorities are beginning to remember amongst other things their railings, and this makes the moment propitious for the consideration of what might be called the *theory of hazards*. Fencing is a way of creating hazards, but hazards are of many kinds. Sometimes they are merely moral, as when a piece of mown grass is surrounded by a stone kerb with the unwritten command 'Keep off'. Where space and distance are wanted this is an acceptable form, though the acceptance of the moral hazard assumes a society with a desire to honour conventions. More practical expedients are the ha-ha and the water hazard, but there are cases in which the practical as well as the scenic requirements demand a visual obstacle or a sense of enclosure, and here railings or walls may actually be an asset to the scene. The notes that follow try not to lay down general principles but to explore the visual possibilities of the hazard regarded as a component of the urban scene and as one of the many tricks in the box of tricks of the visual planner.

railings

Since salvage-time when nearly every square lost its original cast-iron railings, many changes have occurred. First there were the shelters, surface or semi-submerged, then grass gave way to large tracts of mud. With the war's end the forces of privilege once more asserted themselves in the form of chicken wire and chestnut palings. In many cases, however, although ownership was unchanged, those for whom the privileges were kept had gone. Offices, embassies, clubs, schools and flat-dwellers had replaced them. In very few cases have the owners yet caught up with the new requirements that a changing society and its consequent shifts in urban population have brought about. Once the new demands on squares are realized, certain problems will arise as to their planning and upkeep. On the following pages proposals are made which closely affect both these problems.

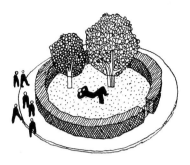

planting

The important thing about the hedge or shrub as a hazard is that it should be an uncompromisingly physical obstruction. Allow a thinness to develop underneath, and dogs, to whom the moral side of this subject cannot be expected to appeal, will play havoc with the landscapist's good intentions. A careful choice of plant species is essential in the first place, and in the second proper upkeep and attention. The planted hazard's thick green walls will effectively screen the secluded inner heart so that whatever pleasure the landscapist has provided there will come as a surprise, which, in itself, is an important part of the English landscape technique.

On the right Belgrave Square after the removal of the railings and before the austerity fencing was put up. This good thick 'woodland' hedge, kept in check by the railings and growing out above head level, would have been quite an adequate safe-guard—so long as it had received the proper atten-tion—to the amenities of the square. It made at the time a real contribution to urban landscape—thick planting, growing out and not trimmed to the muni-cipal gardener's conception of the ornamental.

Left: part of the sweeping railings of Bedford Square. A good example of a physical hazard, well-designed and, in this case, well worth retaining.

concealed hazard

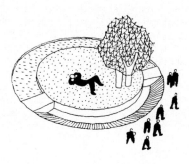

This hazard with an illustrious past has been almost entirely ignored in the twentieth century. Developed for enjoyment of the sweeping vista, the ha-ha, substituted for the garden wall or hedge, revealed that all nature was a garden and, what was gratifying, a *jardin anglais*. What has not been realized and acted upon is the fact that the ha-ha, dry or wet, is equally effective for the limited vista as for the distant one. It is well suited to solve many of the problems which beset the urban landscape architect. For the unenclosed square, where the concealing mystery of the shrub or raised mound is not desired, it reveals the prize, while at the same time enhancing its appeal, by making it relatively hard to attain.

change of level

A device much used in the eighteenth century to provide additional interest in a flat landscape was the raised hillock. Although in the hands of the imitators of Capability Brown it tended towards monotony owing to a similarity of outline in his mound-clump-belt technique, St James's Park and Green Park in London have some good examples of imaginatively landscaped changes of level. The mound is particularly useful if an area is endangered by the ornamental 'municipal park' atmosphere. As a hazard the change of level is perhaps the most subtly persuasive of them all, guiding the eye and the foot where the landscapist wills, and substituting for the keep-off notice a bank, which most people in a city will avoid like the plague.

The Floor

When the railways came they built their own permanent way linking town to town. Not so the internal
combustion vehicle which used roads and streets
which already existed and doing so swept a special
path for itself through all the towns of England. On
first inspection this would appear a natural development. Inhabitants of towns and villages can still do
their shopping or visit each other's houses. But the
river of vehicles has damaged town life in one of its
less obvious but still essential senses. It has severely
restricted the right of free assembly. To congregate,
to be able to stop and chat, to feel free out of doors
may not seem very important compared to the
pressing needs of transport, but it is one of the
reasons people live in town and not by themselves—
to enjoy the pleasures of being sociable. Whereas the
distinction between in and out doors should be one
of degree and not kind, it has now become the difference between sanctuary and exposure. Buildings
are gathered together but they do not form towns;
one might almost as well build houses facing across
a railway line.

There are two closely related aspects to the right
of assembly: the first is applied to the people who
live in a town and the second applies to the buildings
which compose it. From the visual standpoint the
greatest single loss suffered is neutralization of the
floor, the space between buildings, which has
changed from a *connecting* surface to a *dividing*
surface. It has also changed from a particular to a
generalized surface.

The first reaction of a person who becomes aware
of the value of the floor as potential scenery is to
decorate it. Hence the flower-bedded traffic round-
abouts. Hence also the somewhat arbitrary use of
cobbles to form decorative patterns which, though
not so flagrantly pretty, still originate from a desire
to add decoration. The distinctive patterns formed
by differing materials arise from use. Imagine users
of the floor acting in an instinctive or predestined
manner and then plot their movements. The result
will be a 'movement pattern' in which the use of the
floor is crystallized into shapes formed by differing
colours or textures which indicate action. These will
vary from the use of hazards (rough surfaces) to accepted symbols (zebra striped crossings), and to
nuances which can safely be transgressed except at
certain periodic functions. Further, these patterns if
commonly adopted will provide in two dimensions
the service which today normally takes three.

I have already mentioned that the floor could be a
connecting surface between and around buildings. If
it is to do so it cannot be a neutral ribbon of asphalt
flanked by pavements. It must be considered an
equal partner with the buildings and by the nature
of its levels, scale, texture and general propriety,
produce the effect of sociability and homogeneity.

But it cannot do this without itself having power
to move the emotions (otherwise it remains a no-
man's-land, a dull spot in a bright scene. It is no
good running a slab of concrete between buildings
and, since it is continuous, hoping for homogeneity).
The floor must contribute its own unique type of
drama. In what particular quality does the secret
and uniqueness of floorscape lie?

Does it, as some may suspect, lie solely in the
charms of weathering, wear and settlement? Or does
it lie in the variety of materials, many of which are
now obsolete for their traditional uses? I believe the
essentials lie in neither.

(1) As opposed to buildings, whose volumes and
modelling are mainly geometric, the modelling
of the floor is much more primitive and possibly
more subtle. It is a thin veneer of durable
material covering the most powerful and natural
element in the urban scene: the earth's undulation. This imparts to the floor an austerity
and also an inconsequential waywardness.

(2) Due to the fact that it exists only as a surface
all its work is done in two dimensions. It per-
suades, segregates, emphasizes, joins, divides by
surface pattern. Could there be a more perfect
foil to the precise cubism of buildings than
textured and painted 'movement patterns' on
the deceptive flatness of the floor?

(3) More than any other device in townscape it
possesses the quality of expanse or extension.
This quality can be seen not only in the vast
paved square but in the little flagged strip that
disappears round the corner. The first is the
affirmation, the second a hint.

(4) Lastly we mention materials and make the
point that the work they must do means that
they must have durability and weight. It im-
poses a certain discipline on the make-up of
the floor and it is this which gives to the floor its
final character.

The following pages demonstrate the points on
which this case rests. The illustrations are from one
town, Woodstock in Oxfordshire.

adventure

The justification for this section is to draw attention to the dramatic scenery of the floor and to reveal its independent private life. It is not just something that buildings stand on and cars travel across, it has a character and vitality peculiarly its own, long neglected.

functional pattern

The difficulty of driving over cobbles makes them at once an obvious surface for stationary vehicles. Obvious not to the designer but to the motorist who is not tempted to use it. The beginning of pattern based on function.

standardizing the code

The pavement takes a plunge across the road. Clear warning is given by the path of setts to both pedestrian and traffic. The band of cobbles acts as a warning buffer between flagstone and tarmac. Just one example of how varied materials could, if standardized, give a visual Highway Code, establishing conventions, behaviours and frontiers.

materials

A coherent scene but composed of seven different elements unified by a common surface, and clarity of function. Cobbles are suppressed in the shopping area, on the wall side of the pavement, to allow more elasticity of movement and use.

articulation

Articulation of movement by intensifying the contrast of surface and introducing directional techniques. The street is the same but the shops have given way to houses—so cobbles return to each side of the paving. The result establishes the independence of the floor from buildings.

relax

The not-too-urban scene in which we see the two aspects of free assembly for people and for buildings. The small, free path is set in a buffer zone; its casual gutters, its trees in the roadway express the informal domestic nature of the neighbourhood. Contrast this with the dullards' solution, the standard layout applied abstractedly to all streets, urban or otherwise, allowing no tolerances and reducing all urban variations to uniformity.

Prairie Planning

If I were asked to define townscape I would say that one building is architecture but two buildings is townscape. For as soon as two buildings are juxtaposed the art of townscape is released. Such problems as the relationship between the buildings and the space between the buildings immediately assume importance. Multiply this to the size of a town and you have the art of environment; the possibilities of relationship increase, manoeuvres and ploys proliferate. Even a small congregation of buildings can produce drama and spatial stimulation. But looking at the kind of towns and housing estates built by speculators or local authorities one is forced to conclude that this conception of townscape has not been considered (to put it very mildly). We are still in the elementary stage where the individual building is the be-all and the end-all of planning. If buildings are the letters of the alphabet they are not used to make coherent words but to utter the monotonous desolate cries of AAAAA! or OOOOO! What of the new towns designed by contemporary architects to break the bad old AAAA-OOOO stranglehold? Here they are viewed against this yardstick.

2

3

1

Opposite page: a victim of prairie planning traces out his public protest, the reminder of a properly concentrated town.

Open country is the goal of the victim of industrial squalor, with the dream house, 1, that sits in it, framed by trees that lean down low over the nine bean rows to the radio strains of Bless this House. Architecture . . . impeccable if traditional.

Here we see the birth of a street full of such houses. 2, Sish Lane, Stevenage, as it was and still is beyond the development line. 3, the new alignment appears . . . and with it the magic fades as the dream houses 4, multiply to the horizon. AAAA . . . OOOO . . . What has happened?

5

6

7

8

The character that develops from isolationism can be appreciated from the air view of part of the Adeyfield neighbourhood of Hemel Hempstead New Town, 5, which shows so generous a use, or rather un-use, of land that the unfortunate housewife is reduced to using *travelling shops*, 6, for her shopping. One can understand these being necessary in the Canadian prairie, but in a small English town what can they signify except that the scale of development has got completely out of hand—or rather out of foot? Another by-product of this same giantism of scale is the problem of what to do with all the land that isn't built on, 7 (Stevenage). Roads?—roads only need to be narrow. Pavements then?—if the streets are narrow the pavements must be vast— vast enough for all the shoppers of Oxford Street; but at ten shillings a square yard? Surely not. Grass them?—but grass has to be cut. Flower beds?— upkeep again, 8 (Hemel).

Alas whatever it is the main impression of prairie

9

planning is that of *vastness*, the feeling that the little two-storey houses are far too puny and temporary to match up to the monumental, overpowering space. The last thing it does is suggest a stroll; the unhappy pedestrian is left with a feeling of hopelessness in face of a terrifying infinity of wideness punctuated at intervals by seas of concrete. It must be made clear that the carping note of these observations is not directed at architects, since in the main the buildings themselves are successful, and in the layout the architects are the victims of their committees who have somehow got this bee of dispersal into their bonnets—the idea that it is not quite nice to have a neighbour, that the ideal town is one that will fill—or empty—a prairie, 9 (Stevenage).

One of the essential qualities of a town is that it is a gathering together of people and utilities for the generation of civic warmth. However overcrowded, dingy, insanitary and airless the old towns may be most of them retain this quality, which is the essential quality without which a town is no town, *with* which lack of air is merely a minor nuisance— let us call it towniness. Where has it got to in the new towns? Or are the new towns merely intended to negative the old towns and so negative towniness? We see no sign of it here. Instead we see the growth of a new ideal at work which might be described as ebbiness—the ebb tide: the cult of isolationism. It is as though the drive to the country has been undertaken by people all studiously avoiding each other and pretending that they are alone. The result is a paradox, the paradox of *concentrated isolation*, the direct antithesis of towniness, which results from the social impulse. Turning from physical isolationism to what might be called psychological isolationism a revealing example is the treatment of

10, 12, 14   11, 13, 15

an old church in Harlow New Town, 10. The
planners have clearly tried to exploit the potentiali-
ties of this existing feature, but one would have
thought that such a building would have been
seized upon as a focus to rouse and rally new
development, providing the kind of rallying point
the church has always provided in English town
planning. Instead it has been isolated in green fields,
when even God asks for no more than one acre; and
all the houses turn their back on it. So much so
that even the nice views of it (though cut off
abruptly), 11, look accidental. Next, a row of shops
in Stevenage, 12, shows how another centre or
meeting place has been thrown to the winds. It is
blandly self-effacing, simply continuing the row of
houses. What should be a point of congregation
becomes an extended line, dispersing the group and
paying homage to the queuing principle. Another
facet of this disintegration can be seen in the
houses at Hemel, 13. Where house types vary, a
relationship develops between the buildings which
may be turned to good use in bringing the scene
to life. One feels that the buildings are in cahoots.
By contrast, when buildings are identical, without
regard to direction or levels, we do not get unity
but a sulky, resentful monotony. AAA . . . OOO
. . . The last example is of the neighbourhood
centre at Adeyfield, Hemel Hempstead, 14, where
we have the welcome appearance of a square which
sensibly contains shops, pub, cinema and church.
Yet instead of the square being the culmination
of the neighbourhood, the centre, hub and vortex,
it is placed to one side avoiding, so far as possible,
a direct relationship with the houses it serves, 15.

16

17

Interlude at Blanchland

The new towns illustrated here are dead against the
whole tradition of English town planning, or any
town planning. English town planning has been
more open than European in the past, but this kind
of openness refutes and frustrates the whole idea of
town. By contrast, Blanchland in Northumberland,
though no more than a village, has evident urban
qualities. Based on the air view overleaf, the following sequence of views has been sketched to illustrate
the essential points.

16, approach. The gap reveals urbanity in the
countryside.
17, entry and the way through is blocked by the
building opposite which suggests enclosure and a
hint of space yet to be revealed.
18, on turning the corner the space surprisingly
extends, terminating in a beckoning black opening.

18

19

20

21

19, in this enclosure we find one side busy with shops and the wide pavement filled with stalls on market day.

20, whilst, turning back, the domestic enclave is revealed.

21, the exit. Again, we are not presented with an interminable vista but by one blocked by buildings.

Compare the two air views on the right, the one of Blanchland, 22, and the other of the proposed town centre of Crawley, 23. The approaches to planning seem to be diametrically opposed. In the first the village centre is treated as an urban space in contrast to the surrounding countryside; it has no trees and it is paved. It establishes itself as man-made and orderly. Furthermore the buildings have been arranged to create a sense of enclosure, of cosiness, and of drama in the progressive revealing of space and use. These things are the stuff of towns. For a more recent example the reader is referred to Well Hall Estate, Eltham, built in 1915, p. 164. The approach at Crawley appears to be a pure recoil from the physical conditions of traffic jams and overcrowding in the metropolis. In this it probably succeeds. And yet of tension, drama, enclosure, surprise, there appears to be none. All the elements are there but the insistence on isolation is such that we are left with what we started with: a collection of roads, trees and buildings. Instead of townscape we have tree worship; instead of punctuated streets, AAAA, OOOO, instead of a conception of the town as a homely, folksy living place where citizens can get together to drink, play, talk, and grow old as partakers in the greatest of all the privileges of civilization, social intercourse, we have ebbiness; the theory that everybody else stinks and so you must have as much room as possible between.

Translated into town planning jargon this quality of ebbiness becomes low-density housing—the results are deplorable—foot-sore housewives, cycle-weary workers, never-ending characterless streets, the depressing feeling of being a provincial or suburbanite in an environment that doesn't belong to town or country, and the impossibility of ever getting into the real country which this suburban sprawl has banished. End result—travelling shops and high rates to pay for acres of unnecessary pavements at twenty-five shillings a square yard. To sum up, the New Towns, except for rather better house plans, have advanced but little on the old housing estates. In the sense that they tend to occupy more valuable land they are actually a step back. Regarded as what their name claims for them, new towns, in spite of all the administrative energy, publicity and cash expended on them, what should have been a great adventure has come to nothing and less than nothing—and so far with hardly a word spoken in protest.

22, 23

Rule of Thumb

The curse of the English landscape is the absentee landlord. The old landlord, the man who created it, has been taxed out of existence and the new landlord, local and national authority, lives in town or suburb. Consequently that sense of personal responsibility arising from a knowledge and love of a particular piece of countryside is missing and is replaced by a generally beneficent but remote control: the difference between a parent and a foster parent. (How often do we come across some village which at once stands out from the general run of untidy, outraged and decaying hamlets by its trim and homogeneous air, and discover that it is still the responsibility of a family.)

Add to this the fact that authority, almost by definition, is more interested in the art of government than the art of landscape, then what happens to the landscape will be the political resultant of the various pressure groups involved. On the one hand there are the pressures arising from the necessity for new housing, power stations, power lines, railway electrification, military installations, airfields, car parks and roads, radio transmitters, mining and quarrying, etc. And on the other hand are the pressures exerted by the preservation groups such as the C.P.R.E.

It is not surprising therefore that authority, in its attempt to resolve these pressures into a single resultant, will evolve certain broad principles which, by and large, work or make the best of a bad job: rule-of-thumb planning. This, however, cannot be more than an alibi for imaginative design. It is carried out by absentee landlords who have only a marginal knowledge of the art of landscape. In the nature of things it is bound to lead to abuse and outrage. Perhaps this can be clarified by a homely simile. Generally speaking the Smith family have a roast of lamb on Sunday. Mrs Smith, however, is a good shopper and if the quality of the lamb on a particular day is poor she buys something else. Mrs Smith falls ill and Mr Smith does the shopping. He knows next to nothing about shopping but he does know they generally have roast lamb on Sunday. Hence he insists on buying a leg of lamb that turns out to be a disaster. Rule-of-thumb shopping is no substitute for skilful shopping; neither is rule-of-thumb planning an effective substitute for the practice of the art of landscape. Fortunately the countryside has not yet been entirely abandoned. There are still those 'village Hampdens' who have humbly studied their own bit of countryside and are prepared to defend it against the steamroller let loose by rule-of-thumb planning. Here is such a case.

Bingham's Melcombe, the Dorset country house, is comfortable and snug. It has great charm in itself and nestles informally in a spacious valley. The fact that it is a scheduled building is an indication of its recognized worth. The valley itself is of great beauty and it also, according to our information, has been recommended for scheduling as being of 'the highest landscape value'. But these are not two separate things, building and valley. If you destroy the setting you lessen the building, and by the same token if you replace the building by a gasworks you devalue the valley. On the owner's land, and closing the view of the valley, a completely incongruous row of villas was clearly visible. He has planted a clump of chestnuts to screen them and so preserve the sense of unity. Battle was joined with corrugated iron.

The next threat, and it is with this that we are here concerned, arose when it was learnt that the Central Electricity Authority proposed to bring a new 132 kV line through the valley, since it happened to be on the route between Poole and Yeovil. As a result of meetings between the three interested parties, the owner, the County Planning Office and the Central Electricity Authority, an alternative route which avoided the valley and passed through more elevated arable country with few habitations was agreed on. An agreement which was subsequently rescinded and at the time this was written that was how the matter rested.

It doesn't make sense. At least, it doesn't make sense until you realize that the local authority is trying to preserve the amenities of Dorset, and all the indications are that the particular rule of thumb applied here is that since pylons are offensive they must be hidden. Consequently they must avoid the skyline and at all costs pass through valleys. You've got to have roast lamb on Sunday even if it poisons you. Quite clearly the power line should avoid the valley and pass along the alternative route. If this is done it will be established that no longer is the uncritical enforcement of rule of thumb to be tolerated, even though it is undertaken with the best will in the world.

Note: rule of thumb lost the battle. The pylon line now runs three miles to the north, well clear of Bingham's Melcombe and its valley.

Top left, the scene today. In the foreground is Bingham's Melcombe. We are looking in the direction of its main prospect which is marred by distant villas and farm buildings. Top right, the owner has planted chestnuts which, in time, will screen these buildings and preserve the unity. But all would be confounded if the proposed power line were to be erected, left. The suggested diversion simply takes advantage of the contours to protect the house and valley from the outrage of wires. The alternative to a valley route is not necessarily a route which clings to the highest ground; it is the alternative to rule of thumb, and it is to exploit the contours and natural features with skill and ingenuity.

View from the garden of Bingham's Melcombe, showing how pylons would mar the setting of an important and scheduled country house.

The pylons accompanying the valley road. Rule of thumb planning ensures that they would be seen by most people most of the time.

View in the valley showing how the pastoral scene would be shattered by the pylons which, incidentally, due to the desirability for straight runs, would clip corners and necessitate the felling of trees.

142

ADAPTABILITY

The pylons would affect this one house, but if it is a choice of evils there are few who could seriously maintain that this is the greater.

The road for a great part of its route is screened by a tall hedge, thus cutting out any view of the pylon behind.

Where the hedge stops the line of pylons would be hidden by the slope of the hill, as illustrated in the diagram. It is this sort of careful landscaping we need in place of rule of thumb.

143

Street Lighting

Here we are concerned with the impact of a modern public lighting installation on towns and not, primarily, with the design of fittings. Naturally it is impossible to disassociate the two since, as in all townscape, we are concerned with two aspects: first, intrinsic design and second, the relationship or putting together of things designed. Still, for the time being let us give thanks to the hard work put in by the Council of Industrial Design on the improvement of fitting design and concentrate here on the total effect of installations.

There are two sides to the problem: the lighting engineer's requirements, the demand of amenity or townscape.

Recent (post-war) installations in Great Britain are based on the principle of silhouette vision or surface brightness of the road. To imitate daylight—whereby the road surface and objects on it are seen three-dimensionally and in colour—being economically impossible the alternative is to use a lower intensity of light, to reflect light off the road surface evenly so that any object on it is seen as a silhouette which the eye can interpret as man, dog, car, hazard, etc. (As set out in the British Standard Code of Practice CP 1004 : 1952.)

The system relies on the even illumination of the road surface; there must be no pools of darkness. To achieve this the light sources must be placed and sited with some accuracy in relation to one another, especially on curves.

Height, overhang and siting begin to have a certain inevitability. Add to this the Code of Practice recommendations relating to mounting heights (of lanterns) for Group A (25 ft.) and Group B (15 ft.) roads and we have in all its authority and inevitability a modern lighting installation, which marches through a town like a posse of soldier ants.

Now turn to the townscape side of the problem. There is an obvious incompatibility between the ruthless and rigid installation and the actual condition of our towns and villages. Broadly speaking there are three demands which the townscaper puts to the engineer.

To achieve: Unity of scale

Kinetic unity

Propriety.

Unity of scale: The installation should be in scale with the street or environment. To flout this rule will result in an installation either drawing attention to itself by reason of its overpowering height or bulk and making the buildings appear silly and doll-like,

or as in the case of Kingsway, p. 146, failing to make that contribution to the intricacy of the scene (which a good installation ought to do) by being too small, and insignificant.

Kinetic unity: By this is meant the unity of movement. Most installations, of course, are in streets which to a large extent express motion in a straight line. But as students of townscape are aware there are many other kinds of urban enclosure: square, crescent, circus, focal point, closure, etc., which express a static feeling. In such places it is important that the installation, especially by daylight, should not disrupt and destroy this static quality by driving a monument to motion through them.

Propriety: There are times and places where it is difficult to reconcile an orthodox installation with the scene at all. One thinks of some new bridge, a piece of reinforced concrete sculpture, and try as one may the orthodox illumination by means of light sources placed on posts seems to destroy the scene. One thinks also of such places as the Radcliffe Camera group in Oxford and again finds it hard to reconcile ordinary practice with the particular case. In other words, as our examples will show, from time to time some solution out of the ordinary is called for even if it means some sacrifice and a challenge to ingenuity.

If, therefore, the townscaper puts these points forward as essential for the creation and preservation of urban values and at the same time the lighting engineer maintains that 'efficient lighting' comes first and no compromise is possible then we have reached deadlock. Fortunately the situation is not static. Even assuming the continued validity of silhouette vision the insistence, in the Code of Practice, of 25 ft. and 15 ft. mounting heights for lamps for Group A and Group B roads respectively appears to be the imposition of a rule rather for the sake of having a rule than anything else. Quite clearly the essential is to achieve uniform surface brightness, not to say how this is to be achieved. However, the system met its Waterloo at Marlborough (Wilts) where a precedent was created. Although the High Street is a Group A road the light sources were mounted at a height of 20 ft. in order to preserve unity of scale at the insistence of the Royal Fine Art Commission. Furthermore, silhouette vision is, in itself, an unsatisfactory form of illumination. If one silhouette is behind another silhouette then only one shape can be seen and thus we get the danger of motorists being unable to anticipate people stepping out from behind buses. But already more powerful light sources are being marketed which approximate much more to normal three-dimensional vision. The advent of these light sources must surely challenge the whole intricate structure of silhouette vision layouts. For the more abundant the light the more flexible one can afford to be with the installation layout.

The moral of all this is now becoming clear. What we put forward is a plea for flexibility. Once the lighting engineer understands townscape, the urban scene, then he immediately responds, he manipulates light. For no one knows better than the engineer just how flexible his solutions can be. To regard the design of a lighting installation as an exact science is, I think, putting it a little high, and results in doctrinaire decisions. To regard an installation as a separate piece of construction to the fabric of the town will inevitably result in abuse and lost opportunities, and to regard the light as being of a different kind of light to that provided by shop windows, floodlighting, private lighting and so on can only result in sterility of scenery.

What we need to do is to integrate street lighting with the fabric and character of the town, both by day and by night, to manipulate light and the light sources in the full knowledge and love of our towns and cities.

1

code of practice

Silhouette vision whereby the surface brightness of the road reveals objects on it as a silhouette is admittedly second best. To illuminate in three dimensions was regarded as impractical; 1 shows the absurdity of trying to achieve normal vision by artificial lighting. Hence the Code of Practice based on Silhouette Vision, 2, and its often brutal and insensitive impact on towns, 3, this is the world where everything is its own law and where nothing is seen in relationship.

2

3

4

5

6, 7
8, 9

the townscape unities: scale

Everyone wants good lighting. We believe that respect for the environment does not preclude good lighting. There are three demands the townscaper makes of the engineer. The first is to observe scale. The idea is simple enough; examples of light fittings of suitable scale to the environment are shown above at Hatfield, 4, Dulwich, 5, and Pimlico, 6. Below: here are three failures, two, 7 and 8, in which the fittings are too large and one where it is too small and insignificant, Kingsway, 9.

10

kinetic unity

Kinetic unity is perhaps more complex to appreciate but of vital importance to the impact of the environment. Left, 10, we see a village scene, the shopping street is given enclosure (a sense of personality) by the re-entrant buildings and beyond the bridge the vista is closed by trees. The scene is static whereas the installation, 11, bores a hole right through it. The kinetic unity is broken.

11

12

13

14

propriety

There are cases where the orthodox installation is not wanted at all, where the purity of the scene cannot be improved by an installation yet light is needed. At the Pont du Carrousel in Paris they have lights on telescopic masts which are raised at night. Above, 12, on the bridge over the Meuse at Dinant the lighting is built into the handrail (see section). At the Radcliffe Camera in Oxford, 13, one would like to see the only possible solution, flood-lighting, 14. All these various solutions will in fact cost a little extra. We expect that flexibility of approach for the vital 5 per cent.

towards flexibility

Once the basic townscape is appreciated then the drive towards flexibility begins.

Marlborough has recently installed 20-ft. light fittings, 15 (as opposed to Code of Practice 25 ft., 16). 17 and 18 show that the road surface can be evenly lit with lamps at varying heights.

15, 16

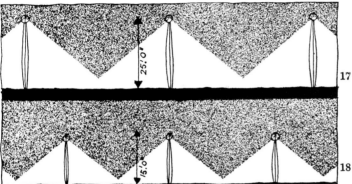

17

18

Experimental lighting near St Pancras shows the use of new and powerful lamps, and suggests that we are moving away from the theory of silhouette vision, 19 and 20.

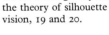

19, before

20, after

flexibility

Below we feature, with pleasure, a model prepared by two lighting engineers, C. R. Bicknell, M.C., B.Sc., A.K.C., F.I.E.S., and J. T. Grundy, to illustrate their lecture on public lighting to the Association of Public Lighting Engineers. Believing that the visual impact, by day and by night, of an installation is just as important as its scientific virtue, they have made their points in this model.

From Vienna we quote Dr Leopold Fink, on the exact placing of lights, left: 'The shadows under the canopy and on the steps introduce the shaping quality and the light on the flowers the friendly element in this picture. Any change in the position of the lamp would spoil this impression. The experienced man in charge of town lighting should know the locations where such effects can be achieved. He will know them when he loves his town and his task.'

21

The two pictures below, 22 and 23, show the same scene with different lighting effects. *From left to right:* Road with 20-ft. columns so that trees can be preserved. Vista closed by stained glass church window. 35-ft. vertical lantern acting as beacon for motorists at main cross roads. Wall-mounted lights on small foreground building. Church tower lit up by sodium fog lamps on traffic island. Square in front of town hall lit by 25-ft. posts and wall-mounted lamps on bus station. Floodlit advertising. Blocks of flats floodlit. War memorial lit from below decorative water. Curtain wall building carries built-in street lighting and is internally lit at night.

22, 23

Outdoor Publicity

One contribution to modern townscape, startlingly conspicuous everywhere you look, but almost entirely ignored by the town planner, is street publicity. Search as you may through the perspectives of the new towns-to-be, and you will be hard put to it to find an advertisement. And yet of all things, this is the most characteristic, and, potentially, the most valuable, contribution of the twentieth century

Above: Strictly to be avoided.

to urban scenery. At night it has created a new landscape of a kind never before seen in history. Strange patterns hover in the sky, enormous signs relay the news, lights flash, stream and swoop, holding the man in the street spellbound, but leaving the planner, it would seem, unmoved. That it must be zoned with discretion goes without saying; that the sort of improprieties shown in the drawings above

Below: Broadway, vulgar
and vital; to be emulated
rather than imitated (see p. 85).

must be prevented is obvious. But to dismiss entirely the whole field of publicity when landscaping new towns would seem to be an act of genteelism reminiscent of the days when the designer ignored everything that didn't fall into line with his own private taste.

The four main objections commonly put forward against street advertisements are:

1. Advertisements are incongruous and therefore injurious to amenity.
2. They exploit the public highway and the public has no choice but to take notice of them.
3. They vulgarize public environment and degrade public taste.
4. They distract the attention of motorists and road users.

It is worth while taking these points one by one, since they can be taken as typical of most of the objections to outdoor publicity in town or country.

Point 1. The White Horse of Uffington and the Giant of Cerne Abbas are incongruous. When you first see them they give you a shock. Yet they do not detract from the landscape, they give point to it by incongruity of scale. But if the White Horse were advertising whisky and the worthy Giant a brand of rejuvenator, that would be incongruous in a different sense. Thus we have two kinds of incongruity, one visual and one ethical. Returning to the city, to Vanity Fair with its busy streets and markets, its theatres and dance halls, the second type of incongruity magically disappears. People still like to buy and sell, to proclaim and to notice. It is part of our

152

civilization. Publicity is accepted as a normal element of modern city life. We are thus left with visual incongruity and surely that is something the townscaper should hasten to accept as a valuable aid. If it is possible for the reader to regard the city as a man-made landscape then let us try to translate the white horses and giants of the hills into a publicity which is just as integral with bricks and mortar.

Point 2. That publicity exploits the public highway is perfectly true but it would be difficult to find other places where it might conveniently be situated.

Point 3. Publicity degrades public taste. But public taste is already vulgar and also has the one merit of vulgarity, i.e. vitality. To put publicity into a strait-jacket, to restrain it, will not improve public taste but simply kill off its vitality. The solution surely is to let the public express its vulgarity, for expression is itself a form of education. In this way the public and its publicity will improve together.

Point 4. Publicity distracts the attention of motorists. In so far as it does it is harmful, and this point must be kept in mind by the townscaper, but the danger is often over-exaggerated by the anti-publicity faction.

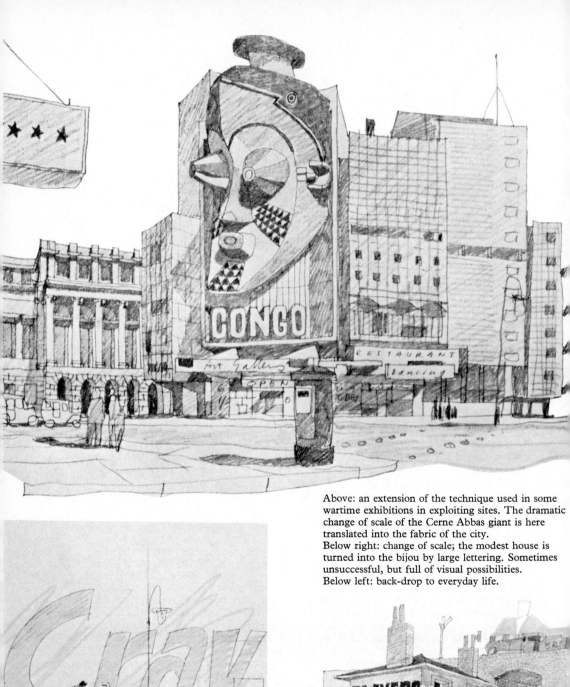

Above: an extension of the technique used in some wartime exhibitions in exploiting sites. The dramatic change of scale of the Cerne Abbas giant is here translated into the fabric of the city.
Below right: change of scale; the modest house is turned into the bijou by large lettering. Sometimes unsuccessful, but full of visual possibilities.
Below left: back-drop to everyday life.

The Wall

All activities conform to some extent to the tolerances of propriety and what we do with walls is no exception. Yet the first aspect of wallscape we come across is the extraction of the utmost effect consistent with such tolerances. Thus, to quote a traditional example, one may see a wall built of flints, the small rounded stones forming a pleasing texture. As far as this wall is concerned the main thing is texture and to this end it is whitewashed, it is not grey or red or blue but *white*, since this extracts the maximum light and shade value out of the texture. Within the limitation of the local builder's materials and the propriety of street architecture this is the maximum effect possible. It will be found true, I believe, of all successful wallscape that this ultimate effect is achieved in one way or another.

This then is the first aspect of display; the second, which may well be but a different facet of this, is concerned with what one might call the challenge of empty space. This is a very simple idea but not easy to explain without running the risk of misinterpretation. The danger is that of being thought an advocate of decoration in which the true significance of a structure is camouflaged in irrelevant surface treatment. The fact remains that the empty surface presents an opportunity, a temptation to those with building in their blood, just as a sparkling white piece of paper presents adventure to an artist. The proper control seems to be found in the emphasis or paraphrasing of function. The diaper, for instance, was probably evoked by its playful but dramatic exaggeration of traditional structure. But today with different methods of construction the challenge of emptiness can be met in other and more appropriate ways. The meander is having success at the moment; it is non-directional and greedy of space and can be applied to the slab building where it echoes the poise and homogeneity of this form of construction.

The mural painting as it is commonly accepted, e.g. the enlarged easel painting, does not come within the scope of this survey although every wallscape is, in a sense, a mural painting.

But, to be clear, in the sense that the word is used here wallscape derives from the intrinsic construction, whether it be the reflections on glass, the pattern of a steel frame or the paraphrasing of construction.

A visual description of these points, compiled from both modern and traditional examples, will be found on the following pages.

seeing in detail

Let us isolate a piece of wall, left, take it out of its context and regard the fragment as a picture. By doing so we may be able to rid ourselves of many of the reactions to wallscape which are more proper to planning or to construction, reactions which prevent us using the painter's eye. What are the qualities of the picture? They are qualities of colour and texture, shadow and pattern and a sense of the inherent strangeness of structural and mechanical shapes.

Where a wall is specially prepared to be looked at, covered with a tapestry or a mural painting, it is generally admired and given attention. If walls are looked at as pictures (as in these illustrations) then to a large extent they become pictures, abstract to be sure, but no longer trivial or empty.

catching the eye

A curious picture, obviously a blatant bit of face-lifting, but included to underline the essential quality of scenic-display in wallscape. It is as though the plastic qualities were determined to be seen—to be noticed—and had burst their conventional bounds offering themselves to the street.

In the following examples the theme of the wall as a painting or a bas-relief is developed with examples which demonstrate the *positive nature* of good wallscape. To find a concise word for this is difficult. Display already has a heavy load of meaning whilst scenery appears too negative for the inventions, the affirmations to be seen.

1, the opposite of drabness—black and white, polished brass doorstep, tile enrichment. This is a gesture to the street, designed to be looked at. It is composed of structural elements and the most has been made of them.

1

2, 3

4, 5

2, the contrast between display and indifference.

3, instead of uniform treatment the wall is made to sparkle by emphasizing contrasting textures.

4, the sunlight pours down, what more simple (if you are thinking along those lines) than to stick a piece of wood into the wet plaster and take advantage of the sunshine.

5, the wall as a tapestry.

6

exploiting the surface

Two examples of invented pattern, 6 and 7, the fretted bargeboard and doorway. By the use of devices sanctioned for this particular time and place, scenes have been created which grip the eye—a roof line, a plinth, a door surround and a pillar in relief. The intention is clear: by paraphrasing functional motifs the empty space has been brought to life. The eye does not slip off but is intrigued, and this not by the natural texture, but by invented pattern. Further examples are to be found overleaf.

7

159

This aspect of wallscape implies a greater degree of visual ingenuity. Here the emphasis is on the primitive desire to fill emptiness, although ideas on what constitutes emptiness have obviously varied during the ages.

Given an empty surface the easiest way of filling it is by the flowing, cursive line reminiscent of a child's scrawl. Not surprisingly the example, 8, is of pargetting, an ancient rural art. 9 is a contemporary version of the same idea from the Paris Exhibition of 1937.

Two examples of the masonry motif. 10, light-heartedly and with small attention to realism, uses the device of *trompe l'oeil* to simulate stone and makes of it a very powerful piece of scenery. 11 is midway between texture and invented pattern, for the joints, being exaggerated, create a linear design which becomes the dominant impression.

8, 9

10, 11

making the most of it

STONE: Gone are the days when stone was used as a load-bearing material on a large scale. Instead it is more often used now as a veneer. Here, in 12, such a wall is presented to view uncomplicated by fenestration or deviation from the rectangle. Another aspect of stone in modern work is its use as a foil to structure, a rich and noble foil the archetype of which can be seen in 13, a traditional example showing two distinctive treatments. Both form lively patterns, the one consisting of stone forming an incident in mortar and the other—mortar forming a pattern in stone.

BRICK: This structure, 14, achieves an effect of monumentality by the insistent repetition of one small unit —the brick—and by very slight movements of projection and recession related to the scale of that unit.

PAINT: Perhaps more than any other finish paint lends itself to the display aspect of wallscape. One of the delights of London is the sight of freshly oil-painted stucco terraces that gleam and sparkle in the spring sun, 15 is in the same tradition.

12, 13
14, 15

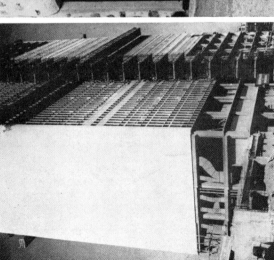

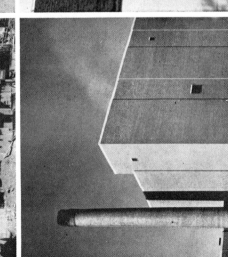

The English Climate

The desire to carry on the normal activities of living in a natural environment is romantic: picnics, camping out and open-air dancing. Despite his beard the gentleman above, who resembles Rameses, is a boy at heart. The city, too, is full of beauty and drama, traffic, crowds, the river and a host of things. But how often do we get a chance to sit and look at them? Contradictory as it may sound a few cities look out, most look in; each little cell is self-contained in English cities, and few English people realize the chasm that exists between their own in-looking cities and the outward-looking ones of Europe, where it is the privilege of the man-in-the-street to sit and contemplate it—in which is contained almost all we mean by the magic word *continental*. The reason lies not in the English character but in the English climate, and nothing much could be done about that, until the age of technics, except to transfer the outside world to the inside as the Georgians sometimes did (at Ranelagh or at the Leicester Square Rotunda). Today, however, there is practically nothing we can't do about climate. The significance of this has yet to be realized. A little ingenuity in our bad-weather-fighting apparatus would bring us suddenly from worst-weather to best-weather addicts, since rain and cloud and gleam of sunshine—not to mention the mist and fog that brought Monet and his Impressionist friends flocking to London to wallow in its effects—become spectacular enjoyments the moment one is freed from the necessity of diving for shelter indoors. This is a particularly *English* problem; it is no good for once leaving it until some American has a bright idea. What is wanted is an offensive (by the specialists concerned) for all-weather gadgets that will make living outdoors a pleasure in the English winter. The suggestions that follow don't exhaust the possibilities; they are more like doodles set down in print to lure the garden—and pier—furniture designers into the open.

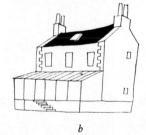

a

b

c

Prototypes *a*, *b* and *c* are familiar English devices for enjoying 'out there', under adverse weather conditions. *a*, is ingenious, but tends to become immobilized either by rust or climbing plants. *b*, is expensive in money and space. *c*, is charming but not very practical, since wind and rain make most of its compartments useless for much of the year.

d

Natural shelters. In a temperate climate the main deterrents to sitting out are wind and rain. Even in winter the temperature is not always so low as to make sitting in still air disagreeable. The question arises, why not construct a shelter that relies on maintaining still air and excluding rain whilst preventing a fug? The contraption shown here, *d*, is

centred on the wind by a vane, so that no draught is felt, and what sun there is will be able to heat by radiation. It is made of moulded perspex with an aluminium vane, fixed on a bronze track; it is suitable for gardens, flat roofs, promenades, piers, in fact, anywhere. *e*, carries the idea further, with radiant heat in the ceiling. The more personal swivel-tilt chair, *g*, like *f*, is in perspex and aluminium.

Air-conditioned shelters. These can be of various kinds. The simplest being a modification of the natural shelter by introducing radiant heat from the roof, *f*, with clean air. On the pier, the park, the South Bank, Leicester Square or Prince's Gardens, sixpence in the slot lets you in for two hours synthetic sunshine, and the rain on the roadway is the ocean providing a free spectacle outside.

Mechanical shelters. An ordinary window may be called a mechanical shelter since one shuts it in very cold or stormy weather. There are many activities, such as dancing and eating, which are perfectly possible in the open in fine weather. Revolving or sliding structures, already in operation at such cafés as the Colisée in the Champs Elysées, allow the maximum use in good and bad weather. For example, *h, i*, a dance hall with revolving wall; *j, k*, a restaurant and bar with sliding walls. On the plan *j*, × × × indicates sliding glass doors; crosshatching, bar or servery; dots, sitting space; arrows, ramps.

Casebook Precedents

If not yet a popular art, townscape could legitimately be called a new art in the sense that it has never been practised before on a nation-wide scale. That, however, isn't to say that its principles have never been applied in this century by individual architects of sensibility and insight. A careful combing out of housing schemes and garden suburbs would reveal the work of a number of otherwise little known planners. Here for the record are two. The first, already singled out by S. L. G. Beaufoy in the *Town Planning Review*, is the Well Hall Estate,

Eltham, built in 1915. The second, built in 1953, is Redgrave Road, Basildon. Though small it is a copy-book example of the kind of peaceful revolution that can be achieved in a bye-law wilderness by a positive visual policy. A prototype not only provides the designer with a yardstick against which to measure his endeavour, it comes as an unlooked-for but reassuring handshake to the designer who may feel he is working in isolation. These examples are just such prototypes and as such qualify for any town-design casebook.

1915 WELL HALL ESTATE, ELTHAM

Architects.
Mr. (later SIR FRANK) BAINE
A. J. PITCHER, G. E. PHILLI
J. A. BOWDEN and G. PARKER

Here the density fluctuates from the open village green to solidly built-up streets producing sudden contrast. This picture shows the unfolding of successive views..anticipation... arising out of the snaking, terraced road. Adding clarity to this is the way in which the street is articulated. The theme is the gable-end; that on the right (projects) marking the curve of the road whilst beyond another holds the eye and then (repetition) creates a geometrical dimminuendo but at the same time avoiding the monotony of a bye-law street.

164

The frank use of (change of level) which accentuates the snaking line gives a welcome variety to the street, (as opposed to the garden on a gradient). In certain parts the houses are built up to the street, a shocking heresy to the splendid isolation school, but one that pays big dividends in producing urban character.

STARKEYS ALES

as it might be.

The estate fails, however, on the score of Multiple Use. There is an overwhelming need for shops or a (pub,) some hint that the people lead a social life. One keeps looking for the awning or the inn sign which never comes.

The pedestrian way is not only a slit left between two walls planned to let people through, it is a series of contrasts, the difference between (outside) and (inside) arousing curiosity and anticipation.

Not a tree was removed from the site and this sketch shows how a (tree) has been used to form enclosure to a section of the road which sweeps round it.

General Note
If bye-laws can be described as legal abstractions formed out of a variety of precedents then we may say that in both this layout and Redgrave Road the architects have put the variety back into the abstractions. For in both cases use was made of waivers on build-lines without which the schemes would not have succeeded.

Chief architect   NOEL TWEDDELL
Assistant architects JOHN GRAHAM
                     JOHN NEWTON
Landscape consultant
             SYLVIA CROWE

The site, as found by the architects, was a typical spec-builder's (gridiron) of roads already laid except for the section illustrated here. The contrast between the spec-builder's layout and that designed by the architects is shown (here.) One can also see the layout of the houses... what do they look like to the user?

The spec-builder's layout, above, produces a never-ending prospect suggesting "I'm a bird of passage". Below is the architects' scheme....

(Projecting buildings) give enclosure and a sense of individuality; a sense of belonging. "I live here"
Subsidiary design points are first, the treatment of road and pavements, second, the use of planting, and third, the use of colour. These are shown opposite.

Although the whole road is read by the eye as a unit, i.e. it is easily comprehended and uncomplicated, yet it may perhaps be described as a chord composed of different notes. There is the differentiation between road and pavement, the latter choosing its (own course) and not irretrievably tied to traffic. In this sketch it is seen suddenly leaving the road and leading to the houses.

To do this it passes through the second element... planting. The hedgerow was left and not uprooted with the result that it provides an extra design element for the architect to deploy. Notice how the footpath passes through the hedge forming a minor pleasure and how the footpath changes character when once (behind the hedge.) Small things which add up to a pleasurable intricacy.

Colour too is used to underline the design pattern, the projecting buildings being painted in different colours to the main terraces.

MORAL
Townscape is seen here not as decoration, not as a style or a device for filling up empty spaces with cobbles: it is seen as the art of using raw materials—houses, trees and roads—to create a lively and human scene.

In this sequence of three pictures we watch building and plant coming togeth
The naked vertically . . .

Trees Incorporated

Trees and buildings have always borne a special relationship to each other because they provide the two standard and accepted ways of punctuating the landscape. As such they have to come to terms. Trees, apart from changing fashions in species, remain the same whilst buildings continue to alter with new techniques and functions. The alteration has now become so great as to demand a reassessment of the relationship between the two. In the past, buildings were conceived as complete in themselves, they contained in massing and façade a variety of richness, modelling, incident and texture which made them self-sufficient works of art. Today the architect seeks to reduce structure to a minimum and the corollary of this is that little but a diagram is left to intrigue the eye. The changeover is shown in the photographs above left: all that was ancillary to the building, even the sculpture, has been pushed out into the landscape—Adam and Eve expelled from the Garden (or rather house). Conclusion: landscape becomes much more important to the archi-

tect, his tight little world of stone and stucco has spread out over lawn and street, pavement and post. Landscape has become part of architecture. The need for enrichment is clear from the introduction by architects of natural stone walls, mosaics, murals and polychromy, and also the use of indoor and outdoor plants, and, of course, trees. Today the art of bringing trees and buildings together is based on the tree lending its richness to buildings, and on buildings pointing out the architectural qualities of trees so that the two together make one ensemble.

The first consideration in working out a scheme would concern the form of composition. Trees are not all green bath sponges on matchsticks, but have astonishing variety. Across the bottom of pages 169–170 are four different tree-and-building effects.

Right, high building and low trees. The effect of truncation can be used to disassociate.

Far right, low building and high trees. The bird in the gilded cage, a contrast of horizontal and vertical.

. . . stressed building obeys its own structural laws and the growing plants suddenly reveal their own . . .

. . . echoing verticality: the fantastic candelabra is like a simile from the structural laws of plants.

Below left, low building and low trees. A made-to-measure effect, small in scale and intimate in character.

Below right, high building and high trees. Peculiarly moving and rhythmic effect produced by the accentuation of the vertical

shadow

Perhaps the most direct and obvious example of surface treatment is the wall in shadow when the tree and building appear on the same plane.

screen

Here the effect of foliage is most important, all the variety of leaves from the feathery tamarisk to the polished eucalyptus. Leaves translucent or opaque, gigantic or tiny.

Free wallpaper is provided for this house of glass in which the wall has disappeared to the extent that it acts as a reflecting surface for the surrounding trees.

line

The calligraphic effects of line vary from the tortuousness of the plane to the tracery of the elm.

geometry

More applicable to tropical countries, where trees and plants display a more direct structure. But the geometry of building combines with the more fantastic geometry of biology.

mobile

The effect of air currents on isolated branches and leaves can be likened to the mobile against a plain wall.

sculpture

Here again there is scope for the specimen, be it one kind or another. It may be chosen as one would choose an *objet d'art*.

Change of Level

The art of manipulating levels is a large part of the art of townscape. Variations in the level of the ground can occur either directly, as a result of the contours of the site, or artificially, arising out of the needs the planner has to meet. But however they are caused, one's reactions to levels are coloured, in the first place, by the peculiar sensitiveness that man has to his position in the world.

Every place has its datum-line, and one may be on it or above it or below it. (There is an opening for misconstruction here, since we tend to take our own datum-line about with us as well.) To be above datum produces feelings of authority and privilege; to be below feelings of intimacy and protection.

These sensations imply a very direct relationship between the observer and his environment. The enjoyment of a feeling of authority and privilege is of quite a different order from the enjoyment of other townscape effects—the sparkle of texture in a wall or the shape of a letter-face on a shopfront. In the first case the observer is committed; in the second he can regard himself as more detached. Yet each is a legitimate and desirable effect to aim at.

Objects acquire significance from their relationship to levels. The would-be imposing building is placed on the top of a slope, just as the statue is placed on a plinth. Hence the difficulty of designing buildings on a slope: there is no datum and the result is often ambiguity. Besides the obvious relationships between buildings and levels there are many subtleties that can be exercised in practice; an example of this is the use of the double order in St Paul's Cathedral, which enables the building to use the skyline of London as a plinth.

The manipulation of levels has, of course, its purely functional uses (see 'Hazards'), but even in the many functional uses of levels there are cases where a choice can be made between alternative solutions, where the problem cannot, honestly, be solved solely by reference to utilitarian conditions. Thus, for instance, one may wish to separate sitting space from circulation space in a park or square. How to do it? By change of level, but whether to raise or lower the space can best be determined by reference to the psychological effect, already mentioned, of being above or below datum.

Is there then any other aspect of levels besides the functional and the psychological? Yes, the third aspect is concerned with the purely visual, or objective, qualities inherent in a world which for many reasons refuses to be flat.

The simplest of all consists of seeing, of being aware of, the undulation of the ground—the cultivation of the sculptor's eye. How many places, which at first glance appear to be flat, reveal on closer inspection the subtle rise and fall which gives a scene vitality? This can be the more easily observed if there is a datum-line against which it can be measured, or a tell-tale—the handrail (see the tell-tale, p. 180) which indicates what happens beyond the immediate horizon.

The fact that a sloping surface is more in evidence than a horizontal one can be put to good use in order to create a sense of space, especially where there are crowds. Visitors to the South Bank Exhibition will remember the grassy slopes which provided such a good foil to the paving and remained green because no one could trample on them. This point introduces the major one of changing level with elegance. The transition is often accompanied by a confusion of unnecessary trimmings—railings and shrubs and the like—obscuring the true qualities of geometry and homogeneity. To regard a slope as vacant space, a visual vacuum which must be made to look pretty, shows precisely the same outlook as that which decorates the traffic roundabout with rockeries.

Changes of level should contribute something positive to the townscape. The point has already been made that the floor is a unity which is too often disrupted, and it may be appropriate to start our survey of levels bearing in mind the thought that although levels change we need not be their slaves.

above datum

Although the phraseology of politics defines a person's position in terms of being left or right or centre, the more usual and natural classification is up and down. We look up to some people, we describe others as having a low mentality. The awareness of relative height is engrained in human nature;

below datum

whether its significance
derives from the primitive
hunt or battle strategy or
from the doctrine of heaven
and hell, it cannot be
denied that even in the
humdrum modern town
awareness of level stimu-
lates the citizen. Height
equals privilege, depth
equals intimacy: the point
made in the pictures here.

above datum

It isn't only the view you get from being high, it's the feeling of advantage, the feeling that you have got into a position of privilege, a position that is just as enjoyable if you look at the view or ignore it. It can be excitingly exposed and exhilarating as in the South Bank lookouts, top right, or more modest, just a raised platform, but a solid vantage, as on the jetty at Minehead, top left. Surely there is something very playful and instinctive in this, for it is just the same as a child's love of walking on walls. The lower two pictures illustrate that both places and buildings assume significance by their position. The raised square at Agde, bottom left, at once appears somehow special, a place worth going to, and the unpretentious buildings in Salamanca, bottom right, situated on what is in fact only a gentle slope, are dramatized by the treatment of channels and steps which serves to exaggerate the change of level.

DEFENSE D'AFFICHER

below datum

By contrast with the area
above the general level, the
area below assumes an in-
timate and cosy character.
It can be exploited func-
tionally to give a sense of
seclusion where it is appropriate, as in the French
street in the drawing
below; or socially as in
that experiment in physical
planning known as the
South Bank exhibition, top.
How right this looks—the
small urban place, made
friendly and concise by its
lower floor.

the tell-tale

We have described the psychological effect levels have on us; here we are concerned with the purely visual implications. And of these the first is the observation of undulation, the vitality which it gives to a scene. Even the floor of a quad gains in interest by being laid to falls for drainage. But the very fact that often the undulations are slight makes it the more interesting to have telltales, the true horizontal which exposes a slight deviation or, as above, Lyme Regis, the railing which follows the contour and reveals what happens behind the immediate horizon. This is the sculptor's view.

changing with elegance

The sloping plane which joins two levels, being unusable, is generally regarded as a dead spot in the scene and too often attempts are made to prettify it. But this example from Stavoren, Holland, opposite top, shows there is no need to camouflage the change; the geometrical precision, together with the cohesion arising out of uniform materials, shows the virtue of the direct solution which achieves a monumental dignity. A different kind of treatment, a fragment from Dartmoor, below, derives its charm from the organic moulding of earth and retaining wall which is enlivened by white paint just where it is needed. Nothing to it? Just a rough wall?

Here and There

On a flat plain a house is built. It is an object standing up on the flat surface. Inside the house there are rooms, volumes of space: but from the outside these are not obvious. All we see is the object. Many houses built together form streets and squares. They enclose space and thus a new factor is added to the internal volumes or spaces . . . the outside spaces. Whereas internal volumes, rooms, are justified in the purely functional sense of construction and shelter, there is no such forthright justification for external space/volume. It is accidental and marginal. Or is it?

In a purely materialistic world our environment would resemble a rock-strewn river, the rocks being buildings and the river being traffic passing them, vehicular and pedestrian. In fact, this conception of *flow* is false since people are by nature possessive. A group of people standing or chatting on the pavement colonize the spot and the passer-by has to walk round them. Social life is not confined to the interior of buildings. Where people forgather, in market place or forum, there will therefore be some expression of this to give identity to the activity. Market place, focal point, clearly defined promenade and so on. In other words, the outside is articulated into spaces just as is the inside, but for its own reasons.

We can therefore postulate an environment which is articulated; as opposed to one which is simply a part of the earth's surface, over which ant-like people and vehicles are forever swarming and on to which buildings are plonked at random. Consequently, instead of a shapeless environment based on the principle of flow, we have an articulated environment resulting from the breaking-up of flow into action and rest, into corridor street and market place, alley and square (and all their minor devolutions).

The practical result of so articulating the town into identifiable parts is that no sooner do we create a HERE than we have to admit a THERE, and it is precisely in the manipulation of these two spatial concepts that a large part of urban drama arises. On the following pages of drawings are some points relevant to this use of space in urban scenery.

here and there

Man-made enclosure, if only of the simplest kind, divides the environment into HERE and THERE. On this side of the arch, in Ludlow, we are in the present, uncomplicated and direct world, *our* world. The other side is different, having in some small way a life of its own (a withholding). And just as the prow of a boat visible over a wall tells you of the proximity of the sea (vast, everlasting) so the church spire turns simple enclosure, below left, into the drama of Here and There, below right.

inside extends out

The corollary of this is the expression of inside volumes externally. In the case of the public house, below, the normal street façade is interrupted by the bulge which expresses the function. Again, the section through the shopping street shows how on one side, the left, we simply have shop windows whilst on the right the awnings and costers' barrows form an enclosure which transforms the whole street from an arid inside/outside statement to a comprehensive and dramatic linear market.

space continuity

Similarly but on a larger scale this view of Greenwich market, above, produces the effect of spatial continuity, a complex interlocking of volumes in which the quality of light and materials denies the concept of outside and inside.

public and private

Emphasizing this difference are the various qualities attached to parts of the environment, qualities of character, scale, colour, etc. In this case the change is from a public Here (Victoria Street) to a private or precinctual There (Westminster Cathedral).

Section through shipping street

shop awnings

Costers barrows

external and internal

A different aspect of space is shown at Kingston market where two similar spatial systems run side by side. First the Market Square, which is entered by devious small roads, widens out into the busy centre which is heightened by towers and statue. The sky is the dome of this outdoor room. Directly off the Market is the Wheatsheaf Inn which also has a central busy area approached by a narrow corridor. This central area has its own sky, a glass dome. In summer the house is open from back to front and in walking through one is struck by this unity of space-sequence.

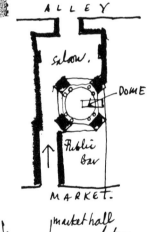

ALLEY

Saloon.

DOME

Public Bar

MARKET.

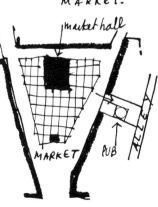

market hall

MARKET   PUB   ALLEY

SKY

INFINITY

space and infinity

The effect of infinity is not normally apparent in sky seen over rooftops. But if sky is suddenly seen where one might reasonably expect to walk, i.e. at ground level, then there is an effect of infinity or shock.

captured space

The carved frets reach out and grip space, the slender rail and posts enclose it, the pierced wall reveals it. Behind, the louvred openings reveal the next dim layer of internal space and the windows complete it.

projection

Space, being occupiable, provokes colonization. This reaction may be exploited by placing space to achieve the desired results. In this view of the Bank of England the lofty portico, left, elevates the spirit more than a lofty solid building might.

functional space

What better way of emphasizing an event in the street such as a theatre, than by giving this function its own space, below, which becomes alive and informed by sparkle and conversation and tension.

deflection

Where a view is terminated by a building at right-angles to the axis then the enclosed space is complete. But a change of angle in the terminal building, as here in Edinburgh, below, creates a secondary space by implication. A space which you cannot see but feel must be there, facing the building.

Immediacy

It may be more prudent to have £50 in the bank than in your pocket, but your pocket is more exciting. Water, sky and buildings are not affected by considerations of prudence. They are there to be enjoyed in the here and now or not at all. There is no Bank of Visual Deposits. The directness of visual contact between man and environment we term here Immediacy, a quality which is on nodding terms with the Victorian practice of Opening Up. The difference between the two lies, of course, in that townscape aspires to practices more organic than was dreamed of by Victorian town-planning, which treated a town as a museum of separate exhibits, a lantern-slide lecture. The key to our modern conception of townscape lies in the fact, the simple but surprising fact, that the items of the environment cannot be dissociated the one from the other. Further, the effects of juxtaposition are in themselves as exciting as the objects juxtaposed—often more so. It is in this light that we attempt to clothe the word Immediacy with its distinct and proper meaning.

Left, Blakeney; below, Iseo

water

Water provides the most obvious example because the transition between it and dry land offers the biggest of all psychological contrasts. Towns that live by the sea should live on the sea in the sense that the visible presence of the ocean should be apprehended from as much of the town as possible. (This doesn't mean always a full view of salt water but maybe the glint of reminder or even a chasm of

space closing the vista at the end of a street.)

For the coastal town the sea is its *raison d'être* and even if the inhabitants live in cosy parlours with their radio sets just like any family inland, it is not an inland town. It is on the edge of the deep, it faces the constant but enigmatic horizon.

The same is true of the individual standing on the quay, only for him the main tension is concentrated on the demarcation line between land and water. It's the emotional experience of this tension which gives the sense of immediacy. This visual and emotional condition may be best achieved by omitting railings at the line of vision as at Blakeney, Norfolk, p. 188, where you may stand on the brink or even *lean out over* the water against the concrete mooring posts and glance down at the boats. Immediacy might be defined as a mental leaning-out-over.

A great deal of the impact of immediacy arises from the degree of contrast, and at Iseo, Italy, p. 189, this can be observed. The hard, infinitely prolonged

edge of urban construction (fixed in urbanity by the lamps and trees) butts directly against the sheet of water. Were all safely wrapped up with railings and flowerbeds, the water would lose its depth and sparkle, the mountains would recede and the wind would not blow as clear.

But there are other combinations, there is the intimate mingling of pleasure garden and ocean at Limone, Italy, above, where the two elements play with each other by indentation and promontories and also by the change of levels: the sea bed rises, the ground is terraced; all views are exploited. More to the point of English conceptions is the direct visual connection with the rougher and more serious jolly-jack-tar's sea, which must physically be held back from the buildings. But the perspective of the hard and absence of railings gives immediate psychological access to the deep, at Limone, left. Here the cobbles imitate wavelets both in their shape and shine, but are as hard as the waves are soft, a contrast which heightens the sensation of proximity.

191

domes

From the most obvious of nature's examples to the most obvious of architecture's—from water to the monument. Wherever one goes in Florence the Duomo is the Inescapable Monument. It is always there closing the vista with impressive sheer physical bulk. It is an architectural personality, a presence as jovial as a fat man in an overcoat, as magnetic and as outsize as a balloon which has made a forced landing in somebody's back yard.

The message of this book is that there is a lot of fun and a lot of drama to be had from the environment. The reader may reply, 'Yes, but you have combed the world for examples. Come and see where I live in the overspill housing of Liverpool or Manchester, in the new suburbs of Paris or the gridirons of American cities. See what you can make of that.'

Agreed. But I have not combed the world just to make a picture book that can be picked up and put down. The examples are assembled for a purpose. The purpose is to expose the *art of environment* which, had it been understood and practised, could have prevented the disasters mentioned. The reason for this book is to reach out to people like you to try to show you what you are missing and to try to implant a growth point of what could be.

Even if you lived in the prettiest of towns the message is still just as necessary: there is an *art of environment*. This is the central fact of TOWNSCAPE but it has got lost on the way, the environment gladiators have cast lots for it and parted it amongst them. On the one hand it has devolved into cobbles and conservation, and on the other it has hived off into outrage and visual pollution. Neither of these, if I may be allowed to breathe it, is germane to the art of environment. And consequently, ten years later, it becomes necessary to start again. Now is the time to fashion a much more realistic tool. Thanks to the aforementioned gladiators the subject is now not unknown. But it is linked to constraints and exhortations. What is missing is the central power of generation. The art of putting the environment together has now to be more clearly defined, its rules stated and its typical products familiarised over a broad field of the lay population. This will be the subject of my next book.

There is an attitude of mind which recoils from the systematisation of aesthetics, believing that the bird on the wing can never be the same when caught. There is another attitude which inclines to the view that unless you define your notes and establish a musical grammar you will never be able to play a tune, even a simple tune let alone Mozart. This seems to me to be self-evident. At the risk of repetition let us get the field of activity defined.

A. The environment is put together in two ways. First, objectively, by means of commonsense and logic based on the benevolent principles of health, amenity, convenience and privacy. This may be compared to God creating the world as someone outside and above the thing created. The second way is not in opposition to this. It is a fulfilment of creation by employing the subjective values of those who will live in this created world. Without disrespect this may be compared to God sending his Son into the world to live as a human, find out what it is like and redeem it. Both these attitudes are complementary. To take a simple analogy, commonweal lines of latitude which are parallel on the map diminish to vanishing points when observed by the individual. There is no moral distinction involved, both observations are true. The truth is where you are. In these studies we shall not be concerned with objective values, which appear to be thriving. But we shall be concerned with the subjective situation which is disturbing.

What we are witnessing is the extreme difficulty of switching from one kind of truth to another, i.e. from the objective benevolence of the town-hall to personal response and experience especially when, in this mad world, there is usually so little time to adjust.

The main claim of TOWNSCAPE is that it has assisted in charting the structure of the subjective world. For unless it is charted to what can you adjust? To opinions, to fashion or to personal morality? How difficult it is to adjust to vagueness and how time wasting.

B. From what base do we set out? The only possible base surely is to set down the ways in which the human being warms to his surroundings. To set down his affirmations. Not the grandiose views on Art or God or the Computer, but the normal affirmations about our own lives. It may help to observe human response to living itself. The baby is born, it has arrived, it is hungry, it cries, it sleeps. It is utterly helpless and utterly arrogant. Later the growing child begins to discern things outside itself, some things are hot and others cold, sometimes it is light and sometimes dark, some big things move about singing. The youth grows up in the family and learns the do's and dont's of family life. When not to ask questions or stay up late, how to get on the right side of dad and so on. Still later as an adult he decides to make his own life, marries and becomes responsible for the organisation of his family.

Our reponse to the environment is very much the same and can be expressed in four affirmations:

1. I am Here, I am in this room, it is now. Awareness of space.
2. They are There. That building is charming or ugly. Awareness of mood and character.

194

3. I understand Behaviour. We walk about inside a web of perspective that opens before us and closes behind us. There is a time structure.

4. I Organise. I can manipulate Spaces and Moods, knowing their Behaviour, to produce the home of man.

All very fine and large. But what happens if we simply brush all this to one side and get down to a bit of designing?

anti 1. There is then nothing to belong to, nothing but waste-land. Non-homes stretching to the horizon and a continuum of emptiness. The Expulsion from Eden.

anti 2. There is nothing to communicate with. We turn this way and that but all is faceless and mindless. Nobody laughs or weeps. We hold out a hand but there is no response from the silent army.

anti 3. An environment as ignorant and clumsy as a crashed gear change, scenery as catastrophic as the implications of a remand home for girls.

anti 4. Chips with everything. Shove in a couple of silver birches.

C. Our first move in creating a system must surely be to organise the field so that phenomena can be filed logically in an Atlas of the environment. So far we have a column of affirmations on the left hand side. Across the top we can set down the differing dimensions of the environment in which they operate. First there is the physical world of length, breadth and height. Second is the dimension of time and third is the dimension of ambience. From these two breakdowns, vertical and horizontal, we can construct a grid or elementary Atlas which, if the premises are sound, should be capable of immense growth.

Having arrived at the concept of an Atlas we now consider the fourth affirmation, that concerned with organisation or manipulation. If we consider the Atlas as a reference library of (visual) words then organisation is the art of putting this word with that to make a lucid statement which is inherent in the particular design problem. And it is this glorious sense of communication that we all need. For God's sake say something!

You can see that it is no more complicated than a cookery book: first you list your ingredients, then you describe how they behave in heat or water or whatever and then you put them together and there it is, a loaf. The only difference between the two is that most people have a lust for eating which justifies the apparently inexhaustible supply of cookery books whereas the environment is, at the moment, a lust-vacuum. It isn't really surprising. The dialogue stopped when they killed off the environmental virtues of Victorian architecture and substituted a lot of personal virtues such as truth, honesty and self-expression. You can see where that's got us, everybody is bored stiff. We've lost our audience. We have to join, separate, divide, conceal, reveal, concentrate, dilute, trap, liberate, delay and accelerate. Throw the ball about, get those stiff muscles working. There is much to do.

Human life apart, there are few things more poignant than the still-birth of an idea in the human brain. Suddenly in the rich humus of the mind an idea pushes up into the light of comprehension. The telephone rings, no we haven't got anthracite grains only nuts. And the idea has gone. Quite often gone forever. The Gods who threw the dice groan in frustration. Our world is continually throwing up concepts, ideas and solutions but a vast amount withers and dies whilst the rest recedes into the paper mountain. What is needed is a frame of reference in which these homeless ideas can be housed: an environmental equivalent to 'Shelter', the British organisation that is privately tackling the housing problem. It is my view that there is an incredible waste of fertility and that this should be halted by the creation of a collecting, sorting and retrieval agency.

And so we end up with a box of concepts and a range of gambits, the whole being co-ordinated and internally self-justifying like a crystal. A weapon with which we can hack our way out of isolation and make contact with the educators, with the mass media and so to the point of the story, the public.